5 Working TO 9

How to start a successful business in your spare time

Emma Jones

About the author

Emma Jones is the founder of home business website Enterprise Nation and author of best-selling book *Spare Room Start Up: How to start a business from home.*

Emma started her first business at the age of 27 (by working 5 to 9!) and successfully sold it within two years of trading. She launched Enterprise Nation in January 2006.

The site is a free resource for anyone starting and growing a business from home. Over 100,000 people visit the site each month to read fresh daily content, watch the home business show, and meet peers in the forum. As well as the site, Enterprise Nation hosts the Home Business Awards, produces the annual Home Business Report and advises the British government on the topic.

Visit www.enterprisenation.com to sign up for the e-news and receive all the inspiration and information you need to turn a business idea into reality.

HARRIMAN HOUSE LTD
3A Penns Road
Petersfield
Hampshire
GU32 2EW
GREAT BRITAIN
Tel: +44 (0)1730 233870
Fax: +44 (0)1730 233880
Email: enquiries@harriman-house.com
Website: www.harriman-house.com

First published in Great Britain in 2010
Copyright © Harriman House Ltd
The right of Emma Jones to be identified as Author has been
asserted in accordance with the Copyright, Design and Patents Act
1988.
ISBN: 1-906659-68-4
978-1906659-68-4
British Library Cataloguing in Publication Data
A CIP catalogue record for this book can be obtained from the
British Library.

Printed and bound by Butler Tanner & Dennis Ltd, Frome and London.
Designed by San Sharma.

With thanks to the Enterprise Nation community.

To all those who post, contribute, comment, and make the site the vibrant and friendly place it is.

"A recession-induced need for cash and an ever-growing infrastructure enabling individuals to act as (part-time) entrepreneurs are fuelling concepts that help ordinary consumers make money instead of just spending it."
Reinier Evers, Founder, www.trendwatching.com

"Many Etsy sellers join Etsy as part-time artisans. What Etsy offers is a powerful channel to market that will turn a number of our spare time sellers into full-time entrepreneurs."
Jesse Hertzberg, VP, Business Operations, Etsy

"Footfall to our stores shows there's a spike after 5pm. The aisles are buzzing with 5 to 9'ers shopping for essential business supplies."
Yetunde Ige, Staples Head of Marketing

Contents

Who this book is for

Working 5 to 9 has been written for anyone wanting to become their own boss, in their own time.

Employees
Looking for a business idea or dreaming of earning a wage from your passion, hobby or skill? Start the business by working 5pm to 9pm, then either keep it part-time or grow it to the point where it's earning enough for you to leave your full-time employment.

Students
Studying by day and eager to earn cash by night (or vice versa)? There are ideas in here for you too. Turn your bedroom into a business incubator and experience the feeling of being your own boss.

Semi-retirees
Retiring from the day job but keen to keep a hand in business and the pension topped up? These ideas can be run from anywhere (including sunny verandas overseas!) and starting them won't wipe out your life savings.

New mums
Looking for an alternative to 9-5, 5 days a week? Look no further. Take an idea and start a venture that can be run in the quiet hours and around school as the children grow.

> *"Looking for a business idea or dreaming of earning a wage from your passion, hobby or skill?"*

Introduction

I recently spotted a new angle to the businesses we were profiling on Enterprise Nation – they were being run in the evenings and at weekends.

People were still identifying gaps in the market or turning a passion, hobby or skill into a way of making a living, yet they were doing so at the end of their normal working day.

Here are some examples:

"I have a hobby which I wanted to share with everyone else. So I launched HobbyThing.com together with my wife. I'm still working full-time as a web developer."
    Dmitri Kartashov, HobbyThing.com, London

"I had the idea for my business after my second child was born. Whilst on maternity leave I developed the plans into a business. I was and actually still am (3 days per week), a sales manager for a medical company."
    Cheryl Kelly, Precious Nappies, Derbyshire

"I hold on to my long-term vision that in 5 years time I will have created a successful and profitable online business which allows me to have a more flexible working life, escape the corporate 9-5, and do something I truly enjoy and feel passionate about."
Paula Green, Kitty and Polly, Northern Ireland

As the comments kept coming, I decided to take a closer look at this new way of working and this book charts what I found. It explains why 'Working 5 to 9' is taking off and gives you 50 ideas for businesses you can start today and develop in your spare time.

Successful 5 to 9'ers reveal how they came up with their idea, how they're marketing the business and managing their time – and whether they're planning to give up the day job! The book is filled with practical advice, tips and links that will guide you from initial idea to creating a business of your own.

I hope you enjoy the book and do keep me posted with tales of your adventure!

Emma Jones
www.enterprisenation.com
twitter.com/e_nation
twitter.com/emmaljones

I. Facts & figures

Working 5 to 9 takes off

In late 2009, over 5 million people were holding down a day job and building a business at night and on weekends. This is equivalent to almost 20% of the UK working population. There are various reasons why this is happening:

Protection against redundancy
It used to be considered risky to start a business yet, in difficult economic conditions, it can feel more risky to stay in employment. When the 2008-2009 recession bit, redundancies mounted, and employees responded by building businesses on the side to safeguard against future loss of employment and earnings.

Extra earnings
Whether concerned about redundancy or not, working 5 to 9 is a great way to earn some extra cash! With research showing nearly two thirds of British businesses planning to freeze or cut wages and nearly a fifth considering cutting benefits[1], it's no wonder employees are putting in the effort to boost their income in out-of-office hours.

Unleashing creativity
Many 5 to 9'ers featured in these pages do something quite different to their day job. Louise Land is an IT project manager by day and cupcake maker at night, Jonathan Dowden offers business support in the day and performs magic at night, and Matt Conway moves effortlessly from bar manager to origami artist. Their 5 to 9 occupations are outlets for their creative talent.

---

1 *'Businesses set to freeze employee pay, BCC warns', Norma Cohen, Financial Times, December 28, 2009*

More spare time!

The UK's Office for National Statistics produces an insight into how we spend our time as part of its Time Use Survey[2]. Their most recent survey reveals we spent 30 minutes less on housework in 2005 compared with five years earlier. Assuming this trend has continued, when coupled with the efficiency of, for example, shopping and banking online, we have freed up time which we can now spend on building a business.

Technological advances

Great technology at affordable prices and within easy reach has made this way of working much more feasible. Throughout the book there are references to hardware, software, applications and gadgets that keep 5 to 9'ers in touch with their business around the clock. Online sales platforms and social networks have been embraced as free or low-cost business development channels to both the domestic and international market. Technology has truly enabled anyone with an idea and some spare time to become a fully-fledged entrepreneur.

It's the best way to start

Having an idea yet needing the time for it to develop and for sales to grow means that starting out gradually is the best way to begin. It's low-risk, low-cost and is a route into enterprise that should be wholeheartedly encouraged.

2 Time Use Survey, http://ow.ly/1pi6H

The indicators

Research and commentators show just how popular working 5 to 9 has become.

In one of the most sophisticated tests undertaken on broadband speeds, in January 2009 it was confirmed that peak hours for accessing the internet are from 5pm to 11pm, when, amongst the usual browsers and shoppers, business owners are jumping online to check orders, respond to customers, network and develop marketing plans.

The number of respondents to the Enterprise Nation Home Business Survey working 5 to 9 increased from 33% in 2008 to 42% in 2009, in a clear sign of working 5 to 9 taking hold in the small business start-up scene.

Online mega-mall eBay reports that the number of Britons with a hobby eBay business grew 160% to 178,000 over the two-year period to January 2008.

Arts and crafts site Etsy.com is home to more than 250,000 people selling millions of pounds worth of stylish products. Research by the company revealed over 85% of Etsy sellers to be part-time artisans.

A poll run on BT Tradespace revealed that 65% of respondents run their business at evenings and weekends. Freelancing website Peopleperhour.com has seen over a third of its registrations come from the category of 5 to 9'ers in the past 12 months, up from only a quarter in pre-credit-crunch days.

"80% of sellers on MyEhive.com are 5 to 9'ers. They make beautiful products, use the site to sell the fruits of their labour and gain a second income as a result. The number of such sellers coming to the site has increased by 20% over the past six months."

Louise Campbell, Founder of MyEhive.com

According to research carried out in February 2010 by classifieds website Vivastreet.co.uk, the number of people searching for work they could carry out in their own homes and in their spare time increased by 142% between 2008 and 2009, with the most popular work searches being for data entry clerks, remote typists, online survey respondents, sales consultants, part-time PAs and translators.

"With millions of people struggling to cope with mounting debt and worries about job security, the option to earn additional income after work and at weekends has proved a life-saver. With a lot of the work requiring just an internet connection and phone, it's no surprise this section of the site is attracting so much attention."

Yannick Pons, CEO, Vivastreet.co.uk

Training bodies are also recording the rise. According to The Coaching Academy, teachers, doctors, personnel trainers and estate agents, to name a few, are "turning to second jobs to boost their pay packets".

Figures from the Academy show a 148% year-on-year increase to May 2009 in the number of people attending the organisation's introductory seminars on coaching. On announcing the results, Coaching Academy managing director Bev James said: "It is the ideal way to supplement the income of your day job. You can work in the day and then see private clients outside of your primary work commitments."

"Thousands of professionals; lawyers, financial advisers, computer programmers and marketing managers are looking for freelance work outside of normal office hours to earn extra cash. Others are turning to hobbies and talents to boost their income and offering tuition in cooking, foreign languages, website design or even pole-dancing."
Robert Watts, *The Sunday Times*, July 2008

It's not just an increase in online trading and business services we're seeing. All sectors are benefiting, including the fitness industry.

Premier Training International, which creates courses for the health and fitness industry, has seen a significant increase in demand for distance learning and part-time courses, with a large number of their 50,000 new graduates being men and women looking for a career that allows part-time working hours.

"There are more students applying to undertake our courses than ever before. 16-24 year olds make up the majority but we're also seeing lots of mums and dads who want to work hours to suit them and save on the cost of childcare. Combine this with the public now being more likely to use niche or specialist services such as personal trainers, and fitness training becomes a perfect part-time occupation."
Debra Stuart, Chief Executive, Premier Training International

There has also been an increase in registrations to become part-time franchisees and consultants, as witnessed by cosmetics party-planning business Virgin Vie. The company is seeing people already in full-time work join the business because of the flexibility and security that comes with being self-employed, particularly in times of economic uncertainty.

The icing on the statistical cake goes to respected trend observers, trendwatching.com. In April 2009 they ran a feature dedicated to the topic of 'Sellsumers' – a descriptive term for consumers who are turning to their hobbies and talents and selling these skills to make money.

The conclusion to be drawn? If you're starting out as a 5 to 9'er, you're certainly not alone!

Data sources
- SamKnows and Ofcom survey of broadband speeds, January 2009, www.samknows.com
- Enterprise Nation 2009 Home Business Report, www.enterprisenation.com
- eBay annual results, www.ebay.co.uk
- Etsy Company Survey, February 2008
- BT Tradespace poll, September 2009
- Vivastreet.co.uk, February 2010
- The Coaching Academy enrolment results, May 2009, www.the-coaching-academy.com
- Premier Training International

Characteristics of 5 to 9'ers

One thing I have learnt in writing this book is that there's no such thing as a 'typical' 5 to 9'er. The successful people profiled in these pages come from across the UK, span several age ranges and cover an incredibly diverse range of occupations. The youngest is 17 and still at school and the oldest is just about to retire. It goes to show that you're never too young, too old, too anything to start working 5 to 9!

Here are the key characteristics of our 5 to 9'ers:

Location

Scotland	7%
North East	7%
North West	5%
Yorkshire & The Humber	5%
West Midlands	12%
East Midlands	7%
East of England	11%
London	21%
South East	12%
South West	5%
Wales	4%
Northern Ireland	4%

Gender

Male	37%
Female	63%

Employed by

Public sector	48%
Private sector	52%

Working a

Full-time job	78%
Part-time job	22%

Running a 5 to 9 business that is

Related to the day job	27%
Totally unrelated to the day job	73%

In business with another family member

Yes	26%
No	74%

Trading online

Yes	80%
No	20%

Using social media

Yes	100%
No	0%

Planning to give up the day job in the next 12 months

Yes	51%
No	49%

As for financial figures, only a handful of our profiled 5 to 9'ers needed start-up funding to get their idea and business off the ground. Of those that did, the amount was less than £500 and they soon earned that back with early sales. And how much are 5 to 9'ers earning? As much or as little as they like, as they grow their business at their own pace.

II. Ideas

50 businesses you can start in your spare time

1. Virtual PA
2. Online information publisher
3. Book publisher
4. Magazine publisher
5. Author
6. Writer
7. Blogger
8. Social media website owner
9. eBay trader
10. Online store owner
11. Giftware maker
12. Giftware seller
13. Artisan
14. Cupcake maker
15. Cosmetics producer
16. Hair and make-up artist
17. Origami artist
18. Picture artist
19. Furniture maker
20. Jewellery designer
21. Footwear designer
22. Clothing producer
23. Baby wear supplier
24. Toymaker
25. Children's party organiser
26. Leisure & entertainment
27. Musician
28. Magician
29. Beer producer
30. Events organiser
31. Party planner
32. Mystery shopper
33. Image consultant
34. Personal development practitioner
35. Fitness adviser
36. Personal trainer
37. Lifestyle adviser
38. Homestager
39. Photographer
40. Accountant
41. Lawyer
42. Translator
43. IT services
44. Mobile applications developer
45. Software developer
46. Print and web designer
47. Electrical reseller
48. Network marketer
49. Pet care
50. Rare breed pig farmer

1 Virtual PA

"Find your niche. It doesn't confine your business, it specialises it."

Name: Katie Macdonald
Company name: Virtually Does It
Day job: Personal assistant to area director

Katie Macdonald's motivation for starting her 5 to 9 business was based on wanting to make a break from the corporate world and enjoy a better work-life balance. She had been a senior PA for years but was looking for a change.

"Becoming a Virtual PA (VA) allowed me to add a new dimension to a career I already enjoyed. I could combine offering my own bespoke business support service, and follow another love: food. My perfect combination!"
Katie promotes her skills to companies in the food sector; she takes care of the admin so the client can spend more time on their business. She helps food writers with research and tours and offers high-class personal support to chefs. She's even happy to play the role of chief critique and tester for new recipes! Katie says that having a niche helps strengthen the client relationship:

"I want to be as passionate about their businesses as they are. Working with a virtual assistant isn't the same as employing a member of staff – it's creating a partnership – so to know you're supported by someone who is as enthusiastic about your business as you are can only be a good thing."

Katie loves all aspects of food; eating, creating dishes and shopping. She also relishes the sense of togetherness that sharing food and eating creates, so turning this passion into a way of making a living is a dream come true. The focus has also helped Katie refine her marketing strategy and keep promotion costs low.

"When I first set up I didn't think I needed a niche as I considered the skills I had were so transferable that I could support anyone in any business sector. Then I came on to marketing my business and I didn't know where to start. After deciding on my niche market everything fell into place. I have a focus to my business, and a focus which I happen to love!"

Give up the day job?

"Yes, as soon as I have created a client base to generate enough work. At the moment I'm building the business and making contacts during the evenings and weekends."

- www.virtuallydoesit.com
- twitter.com/virtuallydoesit

Name: Michelle Briffa
Company name: Paragon Virtual Assistance
Day job: PA at insurance company

Michelle set up her business after going part-time in her role as a PA at an insurance company. She completed a course on how to be a virtual assistant, and in-between tutorials and her job, organised a website and started to secure clients.

"I've spent the last 20 years juggling a full-time job with family life so when I saw an opportunity to capitalise on my good organisational skills and more easily combine working with family life, I jumped at the chance. Now

I'm juggling clients, a part-time job and my family but I'm much happier because I'm in control, and it only takes a few seconds to get to the office!"

The website is Michelle's main marketing tool alongside online and face-to-face networking. She has profiles on LinkedIn, Twitter, and Ecademy and has gained new business from all of them. She's also joined a local networking group. That's a lot of exposure for relatively little outlay.

"My initial start-up costs were low and thankfully I've already recouped 90% of them."

As she is her business, Michelle realised it would be important to stay fit and healthy so hired a personal trainer who handily also coaches on time management and planning.

"We always talk about the week ahead and how to improve it, looking at what could be done better, smarter, quicker, etc. I now apply this approach to all aspects of my life (health, work, family, business and job) and it has helped me to achieve my goals and remain positive."

Technology also plays a key role in ensuring Michelle works efficiently. She is a Skype user, as being virtual means clients need as many ways as possible of staying in touch, and a smartphone means Michelle is able to keep in touch on the move, respond to work requests, and access her clients' diaries and files.

Give up the day job?

"My aim is to be able to grow my client base sufficiently within the next few months to enable me to work 9 to 5 from my home office and move away from paid employment and the 5 to 9 scenario. With lots of potential contracts in the pipeline I will hopefully stay on track."

- www.paragon-va.co.uk
- twitter.com/ParagonVA

Michelle was the Enterprise Nation 5 to 9 Home Business of the Year, 2009.

TWITTER

VAs to follow on Twitter

@AbsolutePA
@DeeVas
@DiamondSec
@emmawalker_uk
@JustTooBusy
@KateBacon
@OrganisedPA
@SJABradley
@VaTrainingpro
@VirtualAngel
@virtualgirluk
@VirtuallyDoesit

LINKS

- International Association of Virtual Assistants
  www.iava.org.uk
- Society of Virtual Assistants
  www.societyofvirtualassistants.co.uk
- Time Etc
  www.timeetc.co.uk
- VA Success Group
  vasuccessgroup.co.uk
- Virtual Assistance Chamber of Commerce
  www.virtualassistantnetworking.com
- Virtual Assistant Coaching & Training Company
  www.vact.co.uk
- Virtual Assistant Forums
  www.virtualassistantforums.com

Online information publisher

Name: John Batchelor
Company name: ur 1st car
Day job: Automotive engineer

John Batchelor is an automotive engineer with Jaguar Land Rover. He's also the founder of www.ur1stcar.co.uk – a website for anyone who's learning to drive or buying their first car. John's site has the blessing of his employer and he enjoys support from his wife and daughter.

"About 4 years ago I was in a role I did not enjoy and for the first time began considering alternatives to my long-standing employment. My wife was very supportive of this and awoke one night with an idea and, unlike us men, who'd just go back to sleep, she got up and wrote it down."

The original idea was to offer parents a professional car-buying service aimed at young drivers and an online resource for those learning to drive. As the idea developed, they agreed on a web-based advice service so that John could fit the business around his day job. His daughter came up with the text-based name 'ur1stcar' and before long the company was up and running.

"As I was employed by Jaguar Land Rover I sought and obtained their approval to run my business as I felt there could be conflicts of interest. JLR was owned at that time by Ford – not many people have a Jaguar or a Land Rover as a first car but many do have Fords."

The site took shape with help from a graphic designer friend and a freelance programmer who turned John's ideas into reality. With the day job still paying the bills, John and his team didn't have to work to a specific deadline so terms were negotiated that suited everyone.

The site launched at the end of 2006. It combines John's love of cars, his professional engineering experience and his parental concerns about the dangers associated with young, inexperienced drivers. Site visitor numbers are rising and work on search engine optimisation (SEO) has seen the site jump to the number 1 spot in Google for the search term 'ideal first car', which is bringing in more visitors.

John generates revenue from individual commission deals with vehicle suppliers, affiliate programmes for insurance, and Google AdSense. He plans to increase earnings by creating links with more suppliers of motoring-related products and services, as well as advertising from second-hand car sellers.

"I've learned a lot about website structure, website design, SEO and building business relationships but my next step is to make ur 1st car a web business not just a website."

Give up the day job?
"I would like to have that option in the future but there's no rush as I really enjoy the job I'm doing at the moment."

- www.ur1stcar.co.uk

TIP
"Decide what you can do yourself and what you can't and then find inventive ways to get that help at an affordable cost, or even better for free!"

LINKS

Submitting your site to the major search engines
- www.google.co.uk/addurl
- siteexplorer.search.yahoo.com
- www.bing.com/webmaster

List your site in free directories
- www.approvedindex.co.uk
- www.b2bindex.co.uk
- www.brownbook.net
- www.freeindex.co.uk
- www.searchsight.com
- www.ukdirectorylist.co.uk
- www.wecando.biz

For more information on how to help your site appear higher up in search engine results (also known as search engine optimisation) see page 201.

For details on how to turn a website into a web business, check out pages 44-46 and section III.

Book publisher

3

Name: Steve Emecz
Company name: MX Publishing
Day job: Business development director for a software company

Steve Emecz got into books when he wrote 2 thrillers in the late 1990s – one of which was a bestseller and turned Steve into a screenplay writer. His last book was co-authored in 2007, but since then Steve has concentrated on publishing books instead of writing them.

"MX Publishing really started with the launch of *Seeing Spells Achieving*, which is an NLP book for people with learning difficulties. The following year we organised a national book tour across 27 Borders stores, meeting thousands of parents, teachers, and children with learning difficulties. It was then that I decided to expand the business and take on more books. In the last 3 years we've grown from half a dozen titles to over 50 and from 4 authors to 30."

The company publishes books in 2 key areas; coaching and therapy, and Victorian literature such as Sherlock Holmes. Almost all of Steve's authors are introduced by word of mouth but the company has also picked up several new contacts through Twitter and Facebook.

The books are sold through an online store on their own site and through eBay as well as all major booksellers and, increasingly, via social media which directs people to the MX Publishing site. The company secured coverage in a national newspaper and on the radio and subsequently Steve had a number of people asking how to go about starting their own publishing business. In response he's offering a consultancy service, which has already helped two publishers set up new ventures.

"There is no certification but you do need to be registered with the right organisations and apply for an ISBN prefix before you can publish. You need to understand the processes and have some good trade references."

Give up the day job?

"I love the balance I have at the moment with my different roles and I'd like MX Publishing to be my main 'day job' in around 5 years time – my wife says it's going to be nearer 10 but we'll see."

- www.mxpublishing.co.uk
- twitter.com/mxpublishing

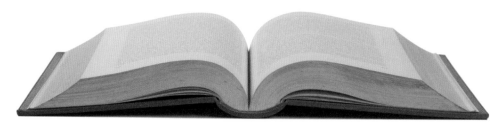

LINKS

- myWarehouse (warehousing and fulfilment)
  www.mywarehouse.me
- Nielsen UK ISBN Agency
  www.isbn.nielsenbook.co.uk
- The Publishers Association
  www.publishers.org.uk (particularly the FAQ section)
- Venda (online store provider)
  www.shop.venda.com

Magazine publisher

4

Name: Lola Bailey
Company name: LifeWest9
Day job: Pharmaceutical educator/trainer

Lola Bailey runs a lifestyle magazine targeted at professional women in Maida Vale and St John's Wood. She started the magazine in 2007 with no previous experience in publishing or media but, having written for organisations on a freelance basis, was spurred on by a love of writing.

"I have a main job which I do 4 days a week and that enables me to do the magazine as it pays the bills. In my lunch break I switch hats and make magazine-related calls that I can't make at night, e.g. making appointments. My husband does insist that I don't work after I get home from the Friday school run!"

As the magazine is published bimonthly Lola is able to keep both it and the day job going. Part of the secret to her success is accepting she can't do everything herself and she's created a network of suppliers and supporters who help make things happen.

"I have a fabulous team of freelance journalists, local contributors, a great design team, an accountant/bookkeeper, a very good sub-editor (who makes up for what I lack in journalistic experience), flexible printers and distributors. I have also taken on a great girl who does the selling; leaving me to do the bits I love."

Lola's experience from her main job has reaped dividends when it comes to promoting the concept of the magazine. Skills developed over years of working in the pharmaceutical industry have given her the confidence to take the magazine to market. She was also helped by joining networking groups that can be accessed at times that suit her.

"Existing clients promote the magazine to other business owners, and I also do relationship building by phone which has worked very well. Local businesses are attracted to our concept of a highly targeted magazine, in their catchment area, that people actually pick up and read."

Give up the day job?
"The plan is to keep both the day job and business going. I'm actually hoping to add to my portfolio of careers by also doing some charity work. As I get more help on the magazine, I can hopefully use any free time to do a little bit of something else too."

• www.lifewest9.co.uk

For useful links on self-publishing and online magazine production, see page 36.

Author

5

Name: Ola Laniyan-Amoako
Company name: Urbantopia
Day job: Teacher

It was through her day job as a teacher that Ola Laniyan-Amoako recognised the small number of black and minority ethnic (BME) writers in children's literature. Ola had first-hand experience of seeing children struggle to identify with the literature available so decided to write the books herself!

"There aren't enough companies publishing books for BME readers and I felt it was time to address the issue. As a teacher, it was very clear to me that lots of readers weren't being provided for. As a child, I felt most books failed to represent me. My books aim to correct this and encourage BME children to read more."

Ola's first book *Leon Spit on the Mic* is about a boy living on an inner-city estate who dreams of being a successful rapper. The book launched Ola as an author and has given her the confidence to keep on with the writing that she enjoys so much.

"Writing is something I love to do. I'm always thinking about characters and possible story lines. Writing is therapeutic for me and is my escape route whenever I have any problems. It takes me to another dimension and provides relief."

ED. NOTE

This book was a 5 to 9 effort in itself!

Whilst managing Enterprise Nation by day, I would steal away to write in every available spare moment.

It took around 6 months to compose the ideas, gather the stories and ensure all the right tips and tricks were included.

I hope this 5 to 9 endeavour helps you with yours!

- Emma Jones

Needing quiet and dedicated space to write, Ola and her husband have converted a spare room into workspace.

"My office is in the box room, which we've split in two, with my husband and I having a side each. It's a bit of a squash, but it helps separate work from home. I can shut the door on it and leave 'work' when I want to spend time with my family."

Ola has just finished a new book called *The Tooth Collectors*, which is a joint project with an illustrator, and completed an adult novel. This author just can't stop writing!

Being a teacher helps as Ola can schedule book launches to coincide with school holidays. She's careful to keep a clear dividing line between her job and her writing.

"I like to keep my work and my business very separate. I don't want to be seen to be making profit from my school!"

Give up the day job?
"That is the big dream. I have been offered a contract as a deputy head so my hope is to complete that and then leave education for publishing."

• www.urbantopia.co.uk

Writer

Name: Diane Hall
Company name: The Writing Hall
Day job: Forensic reports manager

Diane Hall started a VA business in January 2007, offering editing, proofing and secretarial services alongside her employment. In April 2009 she refocused the business and relaunched as The Writing Hall to concentrate on what she'd always wanted to do: writing. The company now offers proofreading and editing services as well as one-to-one coaching to help writers improve their literacy and expression.

"I work in paid employment 4 days a week, run a house and have a family so have to be a meticulous juggler to fit everything in and maintain my high standards. I work in the evenings when the kids are in bed and on my day off whilst they are at school. Sometimes, if the work dictates, I work at the weekends but this is usually in the afternoon once we have had a lazy family morning together and the kids have gone out and about with their friends."

Diane promotes the company in a variety of ways. She offers her services for free to someone who provides marketing services in return, and routinely pays for Google and Facebook advertising (the latter involves running a fan page). By far the most effective promotional tool has been recommendations from satisfied customers. Diane has a 100% payment record

TIP

"As long as you treat your clients with honesty, offer a good service and are a help to them, they will understand when family things come first. If you are the one they want, they will wait for you."

and regularly receives monetary 'tips' for doing such a great job; something which is not common in her line of business.

"My efficiency rules are: no matter when you are doing your clients' work – out of hours or not – they must think you have dropped everything to help them, and if you can't, then be honest when setting deadlines."

Diane uses technology to ensure she's available to clients and her smartphone is invaluable when out and about as she can acknowledge receipt of emails.

"Because my hours of work are so erratic, I make sure I'm contactable in some way most of the time. I have taken calls in the strangest of places! But if it really is a bad time every method of technology has an 'off' button, which puts me in control of my business, not the other way round."

Give up the day job?
"I would love to build up enough work to be completely self-employed, and probably could do so, but at the moment I'm at full capacity with the hours I have available. If the situation ever occurred that my paid employment finished I would definitely make a go of being fully self-employed, but I can't afford to take that decision for myself yet."

* www.thewritinghall.co.uk
* twitter.com/thewritinghall

Name: Alan Law
Company name: Give-a-song
Day job: SEO specialist

Alan Law began Give-a-song.com in late 2004 after his wife came up with the idea. "I had written and recorded some songs for her, and she suggested I try out my songwriting service on eBay. So I did – and sold my first song. I did some more via eBay, until it was doing well enough to warrant its own website – et voila!"

Alan attracts most of his customers through natural, i.e. standard, searches (this is where skills from the day job of being an SEO specialist come in handy!). He's optimised the site so that it's visible for just the right moment when people are looking for a unique gift. He still uses eBay as a means of promoting the site, as well as adverts on other websites that often come free of charge.

"Word of mouth and customer recommendations are a fantastic tool – our customers like to play their song to their friends so we get a lot of new business this way."
As the business has grown, Alan has recruited a team of songwriters. They are all freelance and come together to work on projects. They communicate online as this pool of talent is spread across the globe with writers in the UK, Australia, the USA and the Philippines.

Alan can also claim credit for being the writer of our Working 5 to 9 song! *(See page 224.)* *(See page 224.)*

Give up the day job?
"Oh yes, that's the plan!"

• www.give-a-song.com

For information on how to manage a remote team, turn to page 213. *turn to page 213.*

TIP

*There are many
different businesses
which use writing
skills. Have you
thought of:*

- *Advertising*
- *Corporate
  communications*
- *Marketing/PR*
- *Journalism*
- *New media
  copywriting*
- *Speechwriting*
- *Ghost writing*
- *Greetings cards
  writing*
- *Business plan
  writing*

*Source: Antonia Chitty,
Commercial Writing:
How to Earn a Living
as a Business Writer
http://bit.ly/aABLJP*

Useful links

- Association of Online Publishers
  An industry body representing digital publishing
  companies
  www.ukaop.org.uk
- *The Writers' and Artists' Yearbook*
  Find out how to go about getting a publisher.
  www.writersandartists.co.uk
- *Writers' Forum*
  A monthly magazine for writers.
  www.writers-forum.com
- The Writers' Guild of Great Britain
  The trade union representing writers in TV, radio,
  theatre, books, poetry, film, online and video
  games.
  www.writersguild.org.uk

Self-publishing websites
- Blurb www.blurb.com
  @blurbinc
- Lulu www.lulu.com
  @luludotcom
- Newspaper Club www.newspaperclub.co.uk
- The Twitter Times www.twittertim.es
- Yudu www.yudu.com
  @yudu
- Zmags
  www.zmags.co.uk

Blogger

Interiors blogger

Name: Caroline Taylor
Company name: Patchwork Harmony
Day job: Picture editor for *Financial Times*

Caroline Taylor started blogging in October 2008. Little did she know her blog would soon turn into a business.

"I wanted to output my ideas and inspiration about interiors and a friend suggested I start blogging. I wanted my blog to be like a magazine – full of ideas for decorating your home, new products and shops I'd found, book reviews, news on events and new designers, etc. Being from a photography and publishing background I wanted it to be as visually appealing as I could make it with my limited knowledge of HTML!"

After blogging for a couple of months Caroline began to wonder if it would be possible to open her own shop, having been inspired by so many of the shops she'd featured. She had always wanted to start her own venture and found herself investigating how much it would cost. Caroline soon realised trading online was a low-risk option as there was no commercial rent and no staff requirements– all she was needed was a website and some products.

Patchworkharmony.co.uk was launched in April 2009 and Caroline hasn't looked back. She's busy sourcing new products to sell and site traffic is increasing. In terms of promotion, she's a big fan of print media, believing if your favourite magazine or newspaper is championing a new business or product, you're likely to put your trust in it and buy something.

"I work as a picture editor during the day, and then spend all my spare time working on my business – whether sorting out orders, doing admin, replying to customer queries, ordering new stock or, as is often the case at weekends, sourcing items for my vintage section. The best thing about setting up an online business was that I didn't have to give up my day job while getting things off the ground."

Caroline's plans for the future include expanding the range and holding an event so that press and customers can view the products and meet the friends and family who have helped out.

"I've had amazing help. My mum has given her time to produce my Patchwork Harmony hearts and two very patient friends helped with the photography of all my products. They put up with my indecisive nature and never complained about spending another evening in the studio after we'd all already done a days work!"

Give up the day job?
"I would love to focus on Patchwork Harmony full time. I'm currently doing some 4 day weeks at my full- time job to concentrate more on the website. That extra day can make such a difference. I don't mind losing a little bit of salary as it means I get to work on something I love. At the same time I still need to pay the mortgage, so at the moment it works well that I can run the business alongside my job."

- www.patchworkharmony.co.uk
- www.patchworkharmony.blogspot.com

TIP

"Try to be super organised. Make lists of things that need to get done, prioritise and then just get on with it!"

Wedding blogger

Name: Kat Williams
Company name: Rock 'n Roll Bride
Day job: Shopping TV channel producer

Kat Williams took to blogging in October 2007 after she got engaged. The blog started as a personal diary; a way to gather wedding ideas and keep them in one place. "I didn't care if anybody read it and had no real idea about what I was doing. Key words? SEO? Links? Whaaaat...!?"

After her wedding Kat decided she didn't want to give it up, so the site morphed from a place for Kat to gather her own wedding ideas, to a site where she posted links and photographs of weddings she admired. By offering something different from the majority of other wedding blogs, Rock 'n Roll Bride started to get a small following (about 50 visitors a day) and Kat was loving it.

"However, disaster struck in December 2008 when I inadvertently deleted my blog. After crying (a lot) I resolved to restart the site, using a more advanced blogging platform and in January 2009 the new and improved Rock 'n Roll Bride was born!"

The site has grown to a place where over 90,000 brides, photographers and industry professionals come from all over the world to be inspired for their own weddings...in a Rock 'n Roll way. Kat has also managed to land herself a regular writing contract for a well-known photography magazine and has been profiled in some of the UK's biggest bridal magazines including *Cosmopolitan Bride* and *Perfect Wedding*.

"In mid-2009 I began taking advertisers and sponsors on the site. I have various options for photographers and wedding vendors who want to reach Rock 'n Roll

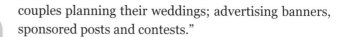

TIP

"Plan and schedule posts. Write entries for the following day before or after work, or on your days off, and schedule them to come up on the site throughout the day/ week. By limiting the number of posts a day the workload is reduced and you don't risk overwhelming your readers."

couples planning their weddings; advertising banners, sponsored posts and contests."

Kat sees the blog as a pleasurable distraction from the pressures of work but agrees her job has honed skills that she's needed to grow the business.

"As a producer I'm in charge of a team of people. Working in such a high pressure, live television scenario has not only sharpened my negotiation skills (great when discussing advertising options with potential sponsors) and improved my time-management ability, but my blogging and writing works as a wonderful distraction. When I get home and switch to 'blogging mode' I instantly forget about the stresses of Shopping TV!"

Give up the day job?
"Most certainly! I really hope that I will soon be in a position to become a full-time writer/blogger. I hope to raise my profile in the UK and open new avenues for me to build income without needing full-time employment."

- www.rocknrollbride.com
- twitter.com/rocknrollbride

Sheds blogger

Name: Andrew Wilcox
Company name: Shedblog.co.uk
Day job: Web developer for media company

Andrew Wilcox (known to his readers, fans, and followers as Uncle Wilco) started the shedblog.co.uk in 2006, having run a website – www.readersheds.co.uk – since 2001. Andrew was looking for a platform to talk about the sheds people had put up on the site and a blog was the solution. It also carries general shed news and items of interest for sheddies.

"The inspiration behind my interest in sheds is a fascination of how we carve out tiny pieces of this planet and claim them as our own."

Andrew blogs mainly at nights and weekends and schedules posts over the week, but if it's breaking news for the shed community he'll make an exception and send an update during his lunch break.

"I also sometimes blog during the commute to work using my smartphone."

Both Shedblog and Readersheds have taken on a life of their own since the creation of National Shed Week in 2007, a national week of celebration for shed owners, with the highlight of the week being the judging and announcement of the winner of Shed of the Year.

With judges including DJ Chris Evans, property expert Sarah Beeny, and well-known inventor Trevor Baylis, the Shedblog attracts plenty of traffic from the week's associated press and online activity. With sponsors secured for Shed Week 2010, this is one aspect of Andrew's income. Other revenue comes from banner advertisements that run as six or twelve-month campaigns and Google AdSense.

"Google AdSense mainly covers the hosting costs and a fresh coat of preservative for my sheds. I promote affiliate schemes for selling sheds on a sister site called Sheds.us, which I'm looking to develop further. It will be a one-stop shed comparison website so people can come to us to find their perfect shed, then of course share their shed on Readersheds to complete the circle."

Give up the day job?

"I would love to work more on the sheds blog but may have to look at developing other niche websites to be able to give up the day job. Watch this space!"

- www.readersheds.co.uk
- twitter.com/unclewilco

LINKS

Blogging platforms
- Blogger.com www.blogger.com
  @blogger
- Live Journal www.livejournal.com
  @LiveJournal
- Vox www.vox.com
  @sixapart
- Wordpress.com www.wordpress.com
  @wordpress

Blogging tips and tricks
- Become A Blogger www.becomeablogger.com
- Copyblogger www.copyblogger.com

Blogging associations
- British Mummy Bloggers www.britishmummybloggers.co.uk
- Crafty Blogs www.craftyblogs.co.uk
- Travel BlogCamp www.travelblogcamp.co.uk
- UK Food Bloggers Association www.ukfba.co.uk

Make money from your blog

As traffic to your blog increases, so also do your chances of generating income. Make a profit from your posts with this top 10 list of options.

1. Display advertising
Offer advertising on your site. The more niche your audience, the more likely you are to attract advertisers. The information you'll need to provide includes:

• Number of unique visitors
• Number of impressions
• Average duration of visit
• Visitor demographics

Write a basic rate card (see page 204), add it to your site and send it to corporate marketing departments and media buying agencies.

2. Google AdSense
This tool from Google does the work for you in that it places relevant ads on your site and earns you money when people click on them. You can customise the appearance of the ads so they sit well with the style of your site. Alex Johnson of shedworking.co.uk uses and likes AdSense but has this to say:

"Unless you get a decent number of visitors a day, then I don't think it's worth putting on. I get over 1,000 unique visitors and my gut feeling is that any fewer than this and you won't be making more than a few pence."

If you get lots of visitors then you could start making yourself a few pounds.

• www.google.co.uk/adsense

3. TextLinkAds

These ads offer direct click-throughs from text on your site. You submit your site to TextLinkAds and then upload the ad code provided. It's your choice whether you approve or deny the supplied ads. Once that's done, you start making money as visitors click on the ads.

- www.text-link-ads.com

4. Sponsored conversations

Get paid for posts (and now tweets) with services like izea.com that match bloggers with advertisers. Some doubt the ethical stance of paying a blogger to write something about a product but there's no doubt that it's a money-maker.

- www.izea.com

5. Affiliate schemes

Sign up to affiliate schemes like the Amazon Associates Programme where you can earn up to 10% in referrals by advertising Amazon products. The programme works by driving traffic to Amazon.co.uk through specially formatted links. You earn referral fees on sales generated through those links. Monthly cheques are sent to you from Amazon and it's easy and free to join.

- affiliate-program.amazon.co.uk

6. Sponsored features

This could include a host of options. Approach advertisers with suggestions of a sponsored ebook, e-news, podcast, webchat, poll or survey. These applications can be added to your site at a low cost yet generate good revenue. For:

- e-book creation try www.yudu.com
- a survey or poll feature try surveymonkey.com
- e-mail marketing try www.mailchimp.com

7. Expert help

Offer your expertise and charge people to log on and watch or listen. This could be made available through:

- Teleclasses – Invite customers and contacts on to a call where you offer your expertise on a one-to-many basis. Check out Karen Skidmore's 'How to get started with Teleclasses' at www.candocanbe. com/products/get-started-with-teleseminars.
- GoToWebinar – Deliver a presentation to potentially thousands of paying customers via www.gotowebinar.co.uk.
- Skype Prime – Use Skype Prime to offer your expert advice and charge for it www.skype.com/allfeatures/skypeprime.

8. Deals with suppliers

Do deals with suppliers. Hosting a travel blog? Agree a percentage each time a booking is made via your site. Hosting a shedworking blog? Create a directory that includes all garden office suppliers but with an enhanced listing for those who pay.

9. Turn a blog into a book

Follow the lead of Wife in the North (www.wifeinthenorth.com) and turn your blog into a book. Judith O'Reilly has seen her blog receive rapt attention and her book released in overseas markets including the US and Germany.

10. Please donate

If you'd rather just ask for a small donation from your visitors, this is possible too. There's a nice example of this at www.ebaybulletin.co.uk, where site owner Robert Pugh suggests, "If you enjoy reading the *eBay Bulletin*, why not buy me a coffee? It would keep me awake longer!" The request links straight through to a PayPal account.

Social media website owner

Name: Sue Hedges and Angela Savchenko
Company name: Moan About Men
Day job: Sue is an exams officer in a secondary school and Angela is a foster carer and teaching assistant

Sue Hedges' husband insists he was not the inspiration for the website Sue launched with friend and co-founder, Angela Savchenko, in September 2007. The site, www.moanaboutmen.com, has become a hit sensation and been turned into a book. From the name, you can probably gather the topic of conversation!

"We find most moans are about habits. I hate to lower the tone but breaking wind is one of the most popular posts, with thousands of readers and replies! Another popular one is the preposition syndrome – putting things on top of, next to, or by rather than in their rightful place! The moans are generally light-hearted and more minor annoyances than serious relationship breakers."

Both Sue and Angie work hard at promoting the site, spending many an evening sitting at the laptop sending out emails to newspapers, television companies and radio stations with funny bits from the site, or items relevant to current news stories.

"So far we have not used a PR agency or paid for our coverage – it has all been done from our sofas with a bit of determination."

The work has paid dividends with TV appearances that led to a book deal.

"We appeared on Channel Five news and were then approached by a publisher about producing a book. At first we thought it was a crank email – we receive lots of those whenever we have any publicity. But when we realised it was a serious proposal, we were delighted. We were involved at every stage of the book, from reading the copy to choosing the cover design – it has been a great experience."

Both ladies are fortunate to have supportive husbands who believe in the business and don't mind the occasional trip away when Sue and Angie have to work on publicity or meet contacts in the evening. On occasion, the kids have gone along too.

"We have found people in the media to be very helpful. For example, when we went on GMTV I had no-one to look after my nine-year-old son, so he came with us and GMTV paid for him to stay in the hotel. When we were filming, the floor manager took him for a tour around the studio – he even sat on the sofa in the commercial break and got all the presenters' autographs! All the children have been in radio studios when we have been recording and have played on their DSes while we are hosting a business meeting in the dining room."

Their respective employers are also supportive and appreciate their raised profile of being associated with a local good-news story. But this entrepreneurial duo may not be in their jobs for much longer as they have firm plans to turn the business into a full-time venture.

Give up the day job?

"Yes. We are working hand-in-hand with a marketing company to do just this. We are planning to add new features to the site in order to become more interactive and increase membership so we can sell more advertising space. While we love our 5 to 9 jobs and have had some brilliant experiences, it would be wonderful if Moan About Men finally became our 9 to 5 job instead!"

- www.moanaboutmen.com

For tips on how to write a press release and get yourself and your site in the media, turn to page 178.

Name: Juliette Dyke
Company name: Fresh Air Fix
Day job: Producer

Juliette Dyke knew she wanted to start her own website and in the summer of 2009 set about researching and refining the idea. The plan was to launch and develop a social magazine for outdoorsy types; a place to meet like-minded people and plan your next big (or little) adventure. The site, www.freshAirfix.com, is up and running and building traffic.

"I worked as a journalist and video podcast producer on a ski website, which taught me a lot about what makes for good online content and communicating via social networks. I also understand what makes a story newsworthy and what journalists are looking for, which helps when it comes to promoting the site."

Juliette communicates with site visitors via an editor's blog and is now planning new features like a searchable directory and booking engine for companies that have been selected to meet the needs of her users. This is how the site will generate revenue.

"However, my first priority is to make great content, build a solid community and develop a reputation as a trustworthy site where users can give honest feedback on products and companies."

Partway through developing the site Juliette changed jobs and now works in the family business for her dad. Being entrepreneurial himself he's understanding, and knows what it's like to juggle a day job and part-time business.

"I've been overwhelmed by how supportive my family and friends have been. I've had loads of free advice in return for a good dinner and plentiful supply of wine, and it's also a good excuse to see them and catch up on gossip!"

Juliette says she manages the job and business by being super organised.

"I make endless lists of things that need doing for the site, and find slots of time either at lunchtime, after work or at the weekend when I can get them done. It helps that my partner is a freelancer and also works funny hours, and that my web designer has previously worked with clients who are running a 5 to 9 business so doesn't mind taking evening calls!"

Give up the day job?
"I would love to get to the stage where I can work on the site full time. I'm constantly getting ideas for new sites so maybe I'll end up with a little online publishing empire! However, bills still need to be paid, so in the short term I'll be sticking with the full-time job and might go down to a 4 day week if things go well."

- www.freshairfix.com

eBay trader

9

Name: Dave Clayton
Company name: Big Laces
Day job: RAF trainer

By day Dave Clayton trains RAF personnel to control interceptor aircraft and by night he runs Big Laces; an online shoelace retailer specialising in fat laces, with a wide range of standard shoelace sizes, as well as sweatbands.

"We originally bought some fat laces from the US in 2006 because I couldn't find them in the UK. It was only cost-effective to buy 10 pairs, so I put the rest on eBay and they sold quickly. I saw a gap in the market so I bought more, then started to expand the colours, sizes, etc, until we ended up where we are now, with rooms full of laces!"

The company started with an eBay store in 2006 and launched its own site to complement eBay sales in 2007. Dave has spent his spare time learning about business, as the skills he acquires through his RAF duties have not easily carried across to his 5 to 9 venture.

"The most important lesson I have learned is to use experts wherever possible. It's really tempting to try and do everything yourself, but there will be certain things you can't do, especially with the limited time available in running a business in the evening. If something is going to take time to learn and/or implement, use that

BOOKS

- *The eBay Business Handbook: How anyone can build a business and make serious money on eBay.co.uk* by Robert Pugh
- *Make Serious Money on eBay UK: Build a successful business online and profit from eBay, Amazon and your own website* by Dan Wilson

time to better your sales, and use that increase in money to pay for someone else to do the thing you can't."

Dave employs the services of a photographer from Australia to take pictures for the site, saving himself and wife Cheryl hours of time trying to learn how to take great photographs and set up backdrops. The company offers a high level of service even if an order is for just one pair of laces, as experience shows happy customers invariably tell others - who come buying too.

Give up the day job?

"I would love to be able to do that, and our income is getting to the point where I could, but having seen what can happen to the economy and with 2 young children, I can't see myself giving it up while the kids are small. Instead, we plan for my wife to assume full control once the children start school and will then revisit the idea when they are older."

- www.biglaces.com

LINKS

- eBay Advice from the experts on making sales: sell.ebay.co.uk/sell @ebay_uk
- eBay Bulletin A weekly bulletin for eBay sellers: www.ebaybulletin.co.uk
- Small Business 2.0 An annual event attracting hundreds of eBay sellers: www.sb20.co.uk @smallbusiness20
- Tamebay An online resource for eBay sellers: www.tamebay.com @tamebay
- Vendlab Advice on optimising eBay sales: www.vendlab.com
- Vzaar Add video to your eBay page/site: www.vzaar.com @vzaar

Online store owner

10

Name: Sharon Brooke and Ryan Smethurst
Company name: Shabean Ltd trading as Urban Africa
Day job: Sharon is an executive assistant and Ryan is an account manager for an insurance company

The basis for launching Urban Africa was seeing African expats in the UK travel home each year to buy items that couldn't be found in the UK, coupled with baggage restrictions that meant it wasn't possible to bring much back. Sharon Brooke and Ryan Smethurst, both South African expats, saw an opportunity and launched Urban Africa as an online store offering 'non touristy' goods that are homegrown and made in Africa, yet hard to find in the UK. They are delighted to wave goodbye to paying excess baggage fees, and to be running a business that starts when the day job ends.

"We've been trading for just over a year and what a year it's been! We've taken part in craft markets and have run competitions via our monthly newsletter that goes to over 700 people; a figure that increases monthly. We were invited to take part in a Namibian radio broadcast and have been featured in a local paper. We've not made a profit yet but we will in year 3. For now we are focusing on getting our brand out there. I started chatting with someone on the train a few days ago and mentioned Urban Africa and to my delight she said 'I've heard of you!' That made my day."

Sharon and Ryan have systems in place to ensure they work efficiently and live happily. The couple has designated an area in the house that's work space, they have a monthly date night and every evening eat at a certain time before working for a few hours and then catching up with each other and the outside world.

"Our family and friends took a back seat last year whilst we were setting up and this year we consciously make time for those people that are close to us. Both our employers know about Urban Africa and we have their support which means it's less stressful than if it was being done on the sly."

Ryan is teaching himself search engine optimisation (SEO) and pay per click (PPC) advertising and the couple also use technology to improve their lifestyle.

"Sky+ has been a godsend! All the good shows are on when we are working, so on Sundays we play catch-up."

Give up the day job?
"Eventually. Our plan is to reduce our product range and focus on items that have a wide appeal so we can sell wholesale as well as retail, and look at other revenue streams."

- www.urban-africa.co.uk

LINKS

- Paypal
  Online payment provider
  www.paypal.com @paypal
- Parcel2go.com
  Choose the best price supplier and send products within UK and overseas
  www.parcel2go.com @parcel2go
- Access Self Storage
  Leave the house clutter-free and store stock with a self-storage provider
  www.accessstorage.com
- Terms and conditions of selling online: A UK government guide to distance selling regulations
  http://bit.ly/9QkuO2
  The Distance Selling Regulations protect consumers purchasing goods and services remotely – by mail order, telephone, online and through interactive TV. The core of the regulations is to give consumers cancellation rights. The regulations allow customers at least a full 7 days (or more time if the seller hasn't provided the right information to the consumer) to view the goods at home before exercising their right to cancel.
- Clickdocs.co.uk
  Ecommerce information and basic terms and conditions available for paid-download
  www.clickdocs.co.uk/ecommerce-information.htm

For information on choosing a template e-commerce website, see page 199.

For help attracting visitors to your store, see pages 178-207.

11 Giftware maker

Name: Victoria Dixon
Company name: Enhance-me
Day job: Mum

Victoria Dixon has turned her hand to a range of roles, from bar work to apprentice jeweller. She settled on a job in administration but having studied art and design, felt she wasn't realising her creative talent. She had been a mum for 15 months when she came up with the idea for her business.

"It started as a hobby. I had played around with image-editing software on my computer, and submitted a few pictures to art galleries, which had sold well. I was then experimenting further and created a portrait of my daughter as a fairy. Having seen this, a few friends wanted similar photographs of their own children. There was such a positive reaction that I decided to put the service online."

Victoria was able to start with no financial outlay. She already had the necessary software and was able to build her own website with the assistance of a very helpful and patient husband who had worked in web design. The business is growing well and Victoria is benefiting from parents who are spending more disposable income on their children.

"The market I serve will always be profitable if you have the right product or service. I mark up my prices every year and order volumes are increasing as I get more publicity. Offering more flexible services to other businesses, such as stock editing photos, has also given me another income stream."

Victoria is promoting her business in a variety of ways; online networking, running competitions, sending press releases to parenting publications, keeping her website updated and SEO friendly, offers and promotions, fresh designs and gift ideas, leaflet drops, and promos in goody bags for various baby and parenting fairs and shows.

"I run everything online which means I can be completely flexible and respond quickly to changes within the economy and my own target market. I have various times during the day (and night!) that I devote to different tasks; emailing, designing, promotion, etc. Planning my time really increases my efficiency."

Victoria is lucky that her 4-year-old going to nursery currently coincides with her 1-year-old's naptime, so (for now at least!) she has 2 hours every weekday morning she can devote to the business in term time.

"I mostly work in the evenings when my children are in bed, which means that apart from checking emails through the day and taking a few phone calls I am able to be a mum during the day and run the business at night. I love that my business enables me to remain at home with my children and not miss out on their early years while still contributing to our household income."

Give up the day job?
(Okay, so Vicky isn't going to give up being a mum but does she plan to spend more time on the business?)
"When both my children are at school I hope to work on the business full time, possibly for 6 months to a year and then decide whether I can make it successful for

my family and myself, financially and creatively. It's difficult to know how much I can expand the business; I have so many ideas but I don't feel I can fully explore them at the moment with such limited time. It really excites me and I hope to be able to make it a success."

- www.enhance-me.com
- twitter.com/enhance_me

For tips on time management, see page 196.

For tips on time management, see page 196.

LINKS

- Hobbycraft
  Gift supplies
  www.hobbycraft.co.uk
- Home & Gift Show
  Annual retail gift shows
  www.homeandgift.co.uk
- International Craft & Hobby Fair
  National craft and hobby events
  www.ichf.co.uk
- Spring Fair International
  Annual trade supplier show
  www.springfair.com

Giftware seller

12

Name: Barbara Steadman
Company name: Another Gorgeous Day
Day job: Finance director

Barbara Steadman describes her life as "numbers by day and words by night" because her day job is finance director at a college and at night she heads home to develop Another Gorgeous Day, which sells gifts with special quotes written upon them.

"I had my light bulb moment in November 2008. At first it was just an idea going around my head but then in February 2009 I visited the NEC Spring Fair to see if the products I wanted to sell were actually available. They were. After that I started to plan. A designer created the logo, the website was developed, products were purchased and the business went live in August 2009."

In 2003, Barbara was holidaying in Australia and bought a greeting card because she loved the quotation on it. Five years later she read an article about the most treasured gifts people had received; many had special words connected to them and Barbara spotted a gap in the market for a single shopping destination that offered a range of quality gifts featuring special sayings or quotations.

Barbara sources the gifts through supplier fairs and is always on the lookout for new products, whether in shops, on websites, in friends' homes or in magazines. Part of this is sourcing items that lend themselves to being printed on, allowing customers to add their own words to a gift, making it even more meaningful.

The business is growing through word of mouth and Barbara also devotes time to marketing and promotion.

"I have put adverts and editorial pieces on social and marketplace websites, I am on Twitter and Facebook, I am networking, I send editorials to magazines and newspapers, enter awards, attend shows and work on search engine optimisation and pay per click advertising. Oh, and I also tell every single person I meet and hand out postcards with details of my website to anyone who talks to me!"

Plans for the future include maintaining a great shopping experience and adding a stream of new products whilst retaining a firm focus on quality.

Give up the day job?
"Yes and I'd love for my husband to leave his. I have set my sights high! Shoot for the moon, even if you miss you will land amongst the stars."

- www.anothergorgeousday.co.uk
- twitter.com/gorgeousday

Five top tips from Paula Green

1. Time is your most precious resource
The time you dedicate to your business is limited and therefore extremely valuable so it makes sense to use it wisely. Plan ahead, set aside specific slots of time in the evening for your business and focus on the objectives and activities that are most beneficial in driving your business forward.

2. Take time out
Take time out between finishing your normal day job and working on your business in the evening. Walk the dog, go for a run, anything that breaks up the working day and then get to work on your business with renewed energy and focus. Take at least one night off each week just to relax, recharge your batteries and ensure you don't burn out. If possible, use some of your holiday entitlement for key tasks where you can really concentrate, away from the stresses of your normal 9-5 job.

3. Set realistic expectations
If you are working on your business on a part-time basis, progress is likely to be more gradual. Do set yourself challenging goals but stay grounded about what you can realistically achieve and when, especially if it is just you running the business.

4. Hold on to the vision
With two jobs on the go it can be easy to lose sight of what you're trying to achieve and why you decided to set up in the first place. I hold on to my long-term vision that in 5 years time I will have created a successful, profitable online business that allows me to have a more flexible working life, escape the corporate 9-5 and do something I truly enjoy and feel passionate about.

5. Expect the unexpected
It's inevitable that your day job will need to take priority. You may need to go on business trips at short notice or take conference calls in the evening or at weekends and this of course eats unexpectedly into the valuable time you may have set aside. This can be frustrating but your day job does pay you a salary and that's the compromise you need to be prepared to make.

Paula Green runs 5 to 9 business, Kitty and Polly, an online gift boutique selling handmade, locally crafted gifts and accessories for women.

- www.kittyandpolly.co.uk, twitter.com/kittyandpolly

13 Artisan

Name: Claire Brown
Company name: Miso Funky
Day job: TV subtitle editor

Miso Funky, based in Glasgow, was born out of founder Claire Brown's need to alleviate the drudgery of the 9-5 work grind. "I started Miso Funky in August 2005 as an antidote to my then day job – something to relieve the boredom of work. A friend and I revisited skills we'd long forgotten – knitting, sewing and embroidery – and then, almost by accident, I created a business."

Claire learned to knit, sew and cross-stitch at primary school but only picked up the skills again when making her own wedding stationery. Claire's aim with her work is for customers to have a stylish accessory for their home and something that will raise a smile when they see it each day.

"My work is best described as offbeat interiors. I take the traditional medium of embroidery and bring it bang up-to-date with a modern twist. The art of embroidery is seen as an old-fashioned pastime, associated with Victorian samplers or grannies stitching pictures of kittens in baskets, but I like to challenge these perceptions with my humorous take on a traditional craft."

Claire's inspiration comes from a variety of places. One of her best-selling items was influenced by a heavy metal t-shirt of her husband and another by a friend's catchphrase.

"I can be struck by an amazing idea when out shopping, at my day job or just from a piece of old vintage fabric. I carry a notebook at all times to jot down ideas for new slogans or artwork."

Almost all the pieces are handmade and with it being such a portable craft, Claire can be found making items at work on her breaks or whilst visiting friends and travelling. The majority of sales come through Claire's website but she also has a presence on online sales portals Etsy, Folksy, ArtFire and DaWanda. Her marketing focus is on driving traffic to the Miso Funky site through blogging, advertising and press coverage.

"Most of my promotion is done online. Simply posting links of new products, or giving a sneak preview of new items helps drive people to the site. I have held a series of giveaways on my blog which has increased readership and encouraged people to join my mailing list. I try to send out a newsletter to this database every few months. I've also started advertising, doing some small banner ad exchanges with other craft businesses. The internet is definitely a vital part in the promotion and running of the business."

Give up the day job?

"I'd love to be able to give up the day job and work on Miso Funky full time, but it's hard to know when to take the plunge. I like being able to fall back on my monthly wage to pay the bills and take holidays when I like! Having said that, I would ideally like to be looking at this as a real option in the next 18 months – as long as I can keep up the hard work!"

- www.misofunky.com
- twitter.com/mooosh

TIP

"Remember why you got into this in the first place and stay true to your goals."

Fashion accessories

Name: Dolapo James
Company name: Urbanknit
Day job: Architect

Dolapo James is a freelance architect and master knitter/seamstress. It's her crafting talents that led her to start Urbanknit, a business selling handmade fashion accessories, with a presence on a number of craft sites and growing sales in the UK and overseas.

By day, Dolapo perfects structures for buildings and by night crafts handbags and purses in bright African prints. She prides herself on new designs, shapes and styles and no two items being the same. Although she had been knitting and sewing for over 10 years, Dolapo didn't turn her talent into a formal business until 2004. Starting with her own website, she soon opened a store on major craft site Etsy.com.

"I soon realised that with Etsy there is a built-in audience so more people will see my work. The same goes for Notonthehighstreet.com, where I also have an online store. I therefore took the decision to link my website to these two stores. Around 85% of my sales on Etsy are overseas, with a large proportion being buyers in the US."

A continued rise in the number of people buying online, and the ability to access these customers by setting up stores on sites without a big layout of time or money, means businesses such as Dolapo's are growing fast. Business is good, as is the lifestyle that comes with it.

"Running my own business offers such great freedom that it often does not feel like work!"

Give up the day job?

"I am at a point where I'm going to have to make a decision about which direction I go career-wise. I think and hope that within the next year I will be running the business full time and, if not, certainly making it more of a priority so that the larger proportion of my time is devoted where my heart is, which is Urbanknit."

* www.urbanknit.com
* twitter.com/urbanknit

Name: Beth Pagett
Company name: Buttercup Buttons
Day job: Student

Beth Pagett is the youngest 5 to 9'er in the book. She's prepping for A-levels and plans to study environmental science at university. Running her own craft business, Buttercup Buttons, will stand her in good stead when it comes to covering the cost of university life.

"I've loved crafting since I was a small child and always used to be doing something creative. As I've got older I've started making things for myself so turning crafting into a business has just progressed from there really!"

Beth started selling her handmade earrings by establishing a shop on a craft sales site. She was looking for an English site and wanted to be part of a strong online community that was user-friendly. She chose Folksy.com and began work on listing a few of her items.

"The forums on Folksy are wonderful. The other sellers are really helpful if you have any questions or problems and I find it easy to manage my shop on there."

Having launched the shop, Beth started to really make a go of the business during the summer holidays by

TIP

"Planning is essential. Set realistic tasks but don't be too harsh on yourself if you don't get them done on time. Starting small is better than never starting at all."

ramping up production and working on promotion. As sales started to build, so did Beth's time commitment.

"I tend to make most of my earrings and promote the shop during the evenings and weekends as during the day I'm either at college or doing homework, though I do find myself tweaking pictures and descriptions when I'm supposed to be doing college work!"

It's early days for Buttercup Buttons and Beth is keeping her options open as to what working life will hold for her once she's graduated.

Give up the day job?

"It would be amazing if I could make jewellery full time, but I really enjoy managing my shop whilst I study, and I like coming home from college to check my shop. I promote it on Twitter, take photos, package and post things, but you never know, I could be doing just that after university!"

- www.folksy.com/shops/buttercupcreations
- twitter.com/buttercupbutton

Top sites for selling

Wherever your handmade talent lies, these sites will help get you started. They offer a powerful sales platform and shop window to the world.

1. Etsy.com

With its tag line 'Your place to buy and sell all things handmade' this is still the mother of all craft sites. Since the company launched in June 2005, more than 250,000 sellers from around the world have opened up Etsy shops and buyers of Etsy listed products span more than 150 countries.

To start selling on Etsy you need to register for an account (requires a credit card and valid email address for verification purposes) and then it costs 20 cents to list an item for four months. When your item sells, you pay a 3.5% transaction fee. This is taken from the list price and is not charged on postage. As producer, you pack and ship the items.

- www.etsy.com
- @etsy

2. MyEhive.com

This UK start-up launched in September 2008 to promote handmade goods, provide instant shop creation, and be an online haven for handmade devotees. MyEhive. com allows you to set-up a shop for free and with no commission. The free package comes with a 5 product limit so you can get started quickly, easily, and with no costs. There are paid packages, which allow you to grow your shop, add more products and images and use your own domain name.

- www.myehive.com
- @ehive_it

3. Folksy.com

The Folksy pricing structure is 20p to list an item plus a 5% commission on all sales (this is taken from the list price and is not charged on postage). If you don't sell an item you are only charged for the listing fee. The site is easy to navigate, has helpful forums, and is home to a growing roster of sellers.

- www.folksy.com
- @folksy

4. Allthingsoriginal.com

A site that features independent British designers. It is free to join and list but you have to apply to sell on the site. A sales commission is charged but the company does not disclose the percentage until you apply.

- www.allthingsoriginal.com

5. DaWanda.com

With sites in the UK, France and Germany, this platform offers free shop set-up and a 5% commission from the sales value (no commission on shipping fees). There is currently no listing fee but the company does suggest this may be introduced in the future, once the site has reached a certain size and number of buyers.

- www.dawanda.com
- @DaWanda_en

6. Notonthehighstreet.com

Started in April 2006 by Holly Tucker and Sophie Cornish, this site offers personalised gifts and other delights you – as the name suggests! – won't find on the high street. At the end of 2009 the company reported 1,500 craft designers using the site with sales of £6.4m. To sell via this site you have to apply and only 5% of applicants are accepted, which means you're bound to be in good company. There is a listing fee and sales commission tailor-made to suit each company that joins.

- www.notonthehighstreet.com
- @nothsdotcom

7. Dreamaid.com

This site allows sellers to sell original handcrafted goods and help artists in developing countries by opting to donate a percentage of the sales price to the dreamaid charity. There are no listing fees but when you sell an item there is a 10% sales fee.

- www.dreamaid.com
- @dreamaid

8. MISI

Created by Emma Hogg in 2009, MISI now hosts over 3,000 sellers. Artisans on this site (the MISI stands for Make It Sell It) sell everything from jewellery to clothing, and prices range from a couple of pounds to a couple of thousand pounds. It's free to create a shop, there's a 3% commission on sales and a 20p listing fee per item.

- www.misi.co.uk
- @Misi_uk

9. ArtFire

This US-based company offers, for free, the ability to sell work across the globe. The cost comes in when you choose to upgrade your account, which is currently $12 (£7.50) per month. After 1 year, ArtFire.com had over 60,000 members and sold nearly 1 million items. Top performing artisans made nearly $40,000 (£25,000) in sales in that year.

- www.artfire.com
- @artfire

10. Coriandr

Coriandr is free to join with a 20p listing fee and 2.5% sales commission. Sellers can also request free promotional flyers where the www prefix is removed from the coriandr.com link so they can write in their own shop's prefix.

- www.coriandr.com
- @coriandr

11. Makers-online.co.uk

The site's aim is to provide "the opportunity for small, motivated designer/maker businesses to develop and grow". All profiles are guaranteed to receive home page presence as the site only takes on a small number of artisans. There is no joining or annual fee, the commission charged on sales is 20%, plus a bank transaction fee of 3%. For this commission the team uploads your products.

- www.makers-online.co.uk
- @makersonline

12. Giftwrappedandgorgeous.co.uk

Launched in early 2009 by co-founders Amanda Charteris and Alison Griffiths after they agreed on the need to showcase British design talent, this site levies a sales commission of 20% with two registration fees (annual and lifetime). The price includes PR and marketing support for client companies as well as a virtual boutique.

* www.giftwrappedandgorgeous.co.uk
* @GWAG_UK

13. Notmassproduced.com

This company is dedicated to promoting European – predominantly British and French – artisans, with all sales being within Europe. Artisans are vetted and the site is by invitation only with sellers chosen for the good quality, look, and design of their products. Artisans choose from 2 packages; a starter pack, which is free, allows up to 3 products on the site and takes a commission of 20% on sales, and the artisan package, which is currently £55 a year, allows up to 20 products on the site and incurs a 10% commission.

* www.notmassproduced.com
* @notmassproduced

14. Joolia.com and Bouf.com

Joolia features jewellery and accessories from hundreds of talented designers with 'big brother' site Bouf.com displaying top quality and unique design items. Sellers can trial the site for free for 3 months and then choose from 3 price packages.

* www.joolia.com
* www.bouf.com
* @bouf

15. Glimpseonline.com

Glimpseonline.com enables designers (jewellery, design, art, and interiors only), most of whom are fresh out of university, to have an online presence. Sellers are vetted before being permitted to sell and there is a 20% commission for online sales and 30% for sales facilitated offline.

* www.glimpseonline.com

Summary of sites and cost of sales

Site	Listing fee	Commission	Other features/ information
Etsy.com	20 cents per item	3.5%	
MyEhive.com	None	None	Monthly packages (£4.99/£9.99) for listing over 5 products
Folksy.com	20p per item	5%	
Alllthingsoriginal.com	None	Undisclosed	Free to join and list but through a selection process. A commission is taken on each sale – confirmed on application
DaWanda.com	None	5%	Listing fee may be introduced in the future
Notonthehighstreet. com	Undisclosed	Undisclosed	The company does not disclose listing fees and commission as charges are tailor made for each company
DreamAid.com	None	10%	Option for a percentage of sales price to go to DreamAid charity
MISI	20p per item	3%	
Artfire.com	None	None	$12 per month to upgrade account
Coriandr	20p per item	2.5%	Can request free promotion flyers

Site	Listing fee	Commision	Other features/ information
Makers-online.co.uk	None	20% plus bank transaction fee of 3%	
Giftwrappedandgorgeous.co.uk	None	20%	Annual package of £260 and lifetime at £395 which comes with marketing and PR support
Notmassproduced.com	None	20% (starter package) 10% (artisan package)	Starter package is free – allows up to 3 product listings Artisan package is £55 pa – allows up to 20 product listings
Joolia.com	None	25%	Free 3 month trial. Three packages, start at £4.99 per month
Glimpseonline.com	None	20% for online sales and 30% for sales facilitated offline	Have to apply for consideration to sell

Prices correct at time of going to print.

- **Shop Handmade UK**
  This is not a site for selling but a directory. The core of the site is a listing of UK-based designers and makers, that helps shoppers find handmade products from UK artisans. A listing in the directory costs £2.50.
  www.shophandmade.co.uk
- **Craftyblogs:** A directory of UK craft blogs
  www.craftyblogs.co.uk
- **Freeosk**: Free-standing mobile kiosks for creative businesses
  www.freeosk.co.uk
- **Glasgow Craft Mafia**: Glasgow-based community of crafters
  www.glasgowcraftmafia.com
- **Handmade Craft Fairs**: A not-for-profit organiser of fairs exclusively for handmade crafts
  www.handmadecraftfairs.co.uk
- **Buy Handmade**: A site on which to pledge your allegiance to all things handmade
  www.buyhandmade.org
- **The Affordable Vintage Fair**: Nationwide fairs
  www.vintagefair.co.uk
- **The Make Lounge**: Offers contemporary craft workshops with a stylish, social twist
  www.themakelounge.com
- **Nottingham Craft Mafia**: Nottingham-based community of crafters
  www.nottinghamcraftmafia.com
- **Project Wonderful**: Online advertising system that matches artisans with advertisers
  www.projectwonderful.com
- **Sheffield's Craft Consortium**: Sheffield-based community of crafters
  www.craft-candy.org
- **UK Handmade**: Stylish, high-quality online magazine with business advice, features of crafters, event listings, etc.
  www.ukhandmade.co.uk
- **We Make London**: A showcase for UK designers
  wemakelondon.blogspot.com

Cupcake maker

Name: Louise Land
Company name: Cirencester Cupcakes
Day job: IT project manager

Growing up with parents who ran their own business meant Louise Land had always wanted to be her own boss, and in early 2008 she started work on her plan.

"I noticed there was a gap in the market for a cupcake maker in the Cotswolds area; there were businesses based in Cheltenham and Gloucester, but no-one had really focused on the Cirencester and the Cotswold villages, so I decided to give it a go!"

Louise had been baking cakes for family and friends for a few years but only started to take it seriously after making a wedding cake for her brother and receiving order requests on the day. She's been baking cupcakes ever since; for birthdays, weddings, christenings and just about any other occasion.

On the sales side, Louise mainly relies on word-of-mouth recommendation. She's starting to take part in local craft fairs and farmers' markets and is making the most of social networking sites such as Facebook and Twitter to promote the business. Louise writes a blog about all things baking-related and her website has been optimised which is helping boost page rankings in directories such as Google, Bing and Yahoo.

"I'm hoping that once I've built up a good reputation I'll be able to start investing in advertising in the more traditional sense, but at the moment I'm having a great response online."

Give up the day job?
"I'd love to, but I'm not quite ready. In the future I hope to go full time but first I have to build up my client base and reputation and then I think a bigger kitchen is in order!"

- www.cirencestercupcakes.com
- twitter.com/happy_food

See pages 77 and 191-192 for tips and links on how to display products at farmers' markets and trade shows.

Name: Claire Melvin
Company name: Claire's Handmade Cakes
Day job: Department administrator for a charity

Claire Melvin has worked in finance and administration for the last 10 years. She has a passion for making cakes and is now turning this into a sideline business. Task number 1: build a website.

"I approached a local artist to create my artwork. I chose the colours and she took it from there. I had an idea of how I wanted the site to look, having researched cake companies and considered what I did and didn't like. I wanted the site to be appealing and easy for me to update."

Claire then approached her brother who has website design experience. He agreed to help and the site was launched. Claire's start-up costs have been minimal

with only an outlay for the website and basic stock for the first order of cupcakes. Task number 2: start-up admin.

"As I've been involved in finance for the last decade, I have an understanding of accounts and figures which has been helpful when corresponding with Companies House and HMRC. Whilst this is not something I need to get too bogged down with now, it will certainly stand me in good stead for the future."

With the website launched and the admin taken care of it's time to start marketing. This is where Claire feels there's still more work to be done as she sets about developing a marketing plan and promoting the business.

"I realise that having a site is of no use if no one knows about it! I have created a Facebook group for friends and hopefully friends of friends. Now I need to sit down and plan how I'm going to get the business out there."

Give up the day job?
"Ideally I would like my 5-9 business to become my full-time job. If I am successful, I would like to open a fair-trade and organic bakery/coffee shop in the area, where I make my cakes on the side."

- www.claireshandmadecakes.com
- twitter.com/claires_cakes

LINKS

- **Farmers' markets**: Display your cupcakes at farmers' markets. First you will need to contact the environmental health officer at your local council to get approval www.farmersmarkets.net
- **Local council**: Your kitchen must be registered as health and safety checked by your local council. Contact them to arrange an inspection visit www.direct.gov.uk
- **Local Food Advisor**: Source local produce, including farm shops for eggs, butter and flour www.localfoodadvisor.com
- **Mumswhobake**: Courses, products and advice for anyone wanting to turn a hand to baking www.mumswhobake.co.uk
- **National Cupcake Week**: A celebration of cupcakes, hosted by British Baker magazine www.bakeryinfo.co.uk
- **Tastia**: A food and drink site for small producers to sell products. No listing or joining fee, but a 15% commission on sales www.tastia.com
- **Virtual Farmers Market**: If you'd rather stay in the warm and sell goods from your home office as opposed to the town square, log on and sign up to the Virtual Farmers Market www.vfmuk.com

15 Cosmetics producer

Name: Emma McCrory
Company name: Rock Face Minerals
Day job: Business consultant

Emma McCrory is a 30-something mum of two boys, working full-time as a business consultant for an IT firm. Whilst expecting her second son Emma started thinking about starting her own business so she could spend more time with the boys.

Emma had been interested in mineral make-up for years and since the products are small and non-perishable she was able to start the business from her attic room and take things at her own pace, without needing to raise finance. She was also keen to do something that was quite different to her day job.

"I'm a business consultant, advising clients in relation to their financial systems. I took a conscious decision to do something different to my 'proper' job and even though my job is in IT, setting up a website and all that goes with it has been a completely new experience. This time last year I had no idea what SEO stood for, or what source code was!"

The site launched in January 2009 and Emma has a growing band of loyal customers. As well as picking up new IT skills she's been learning about marketing and how to promote the business on a shoestring budget. She has run a Google AdWords campaign, placed business cards in local shops and cafés, writes a blog and secured free editorial in local papers that has shown to be doubly effective if it appears online with a link through to the website. Having primarily started Rock Face Minerals to spend more time with her family Emma has successfully involved them in the business.

"I have a video on my blog of my 2-year-old showing the techniques for applying mineral foundation, and my 6-year-old refuses to believe he used to go to daycare wearing eyeshadow that he'd proudly applied all by himself! My husband's main job is to make sure the IT hardware is working and the chief product testers have been my sister, Mum and some of my work colleagues who had never tried mineral makeup before and have been converted in the process. Armed with over 100 samples and a box of baby wipes, my sister and I spent one night testing products to decide which should be included on the website."

Give up the day job?

"That's the plan. I'd like to be able to give up the day job so I can spend more time with the boys and be there for homework and after-school activities. (Though who am I kidding? They'll want to come home and watch cartoons and play their DS!)"

- www.rockfaceminerals.co.uk
- twitter.com/rockfacemineral

TIP

"Keep a little book with you at all times for capturing those brilliant ideas you'll have in the middle of work, or little nuggets of information you discover, or things you need to work on.

"Particularly for other mums: take a bit of time out for yourself and remember to look after your health. Building your business after hours doesn't count as me time. And neither does doing the ironing."

LINKS

- Cosmetic Safety Assessment: Providing safety certification to cosmetic producers www.cosmeticsafetyassessment.com
- Guild of Craft Soap & Toiletry Makers: Focus is on legislation and compliance www.gcstm.co.uk
- Health and Safety Executive: To have home office/storage certified www.hse.gov.uk
- Plush Folly: Courses and make your own cosmetics kits www.plushfolly.com
- Soap School: Soap making and cosmetic courses at www.soapschool.com
- The Soap Kitchen: Cosmetic supplies www.thesoapkitchen.co.uk

16 Hair and make-up artist

Name: Lynn Taylor
Company name: Penelope Parasol
Day job: Hair and make-up artist

It was whilst Lynn Taylor was doing hair and make-up on Hollywood sets that she first came up with the idea for a new kind of parasol.

By day Lynn is a style adviser covering hair and make-up (think Trinny and Susannah with experience of Hollywood celebs) and by night she's developing another beauty business, Penelope Parasol, with the core product being a modern parasol for women that protects skin from UV rays. Having come up with the idea, Lynn worked on securing finance for production and with an American partner identified the key market as the USA.

"I love parasols and whilst working with actresses and living in LA I saw a great need for them. (They are also handy to block paparazzi from getting a shot!) I managed to get my first sample in a shoot for *People* magazine in which actress Ann Paquin is carrying one."

The parasols are UV-coated, made out of stylish fabrics and have a smaller span than a normal umbrella so are highly portable and can be used in a crowd. Through her network of contacts Lynn met someone with knowledge of the manufacturing and packaging process and they, in turn, made an introduction to a credible factory and mill. Lynn is clear on how she wants to market and promote her product:

"I'm going to focus on celebrities and magazines and will be giving the parasols to fashion stylists to use in shoots. One of my PR goals for this year is to get a Hollywood celebrity to carry one of my products whilst being interviewed on the red carpet at the Emmys. These events get enormous coverage!"

The parasols will be sold through high-end stores and websites.

Give up the day job?
"Absolutely! I want to go full-time in the business as soon as it launches but that may change if I get a contract to do hair and make-up for a big film."

* www.penelopeparasols.com

LINKS

* Return to Glory
  Display site for mobile beauty, massage and wellness treatments
  www.returntoglory.co.uk
* Wahanda
  Source for local information on health and wellness
  www.wahanda.com

17 Origami artist

Name: Matt Conway
Company name: Conways Origami
Day job: Bar manager

It was in his efforts to quit smoking that Matt Conway discovered a talent for origami art. His friend, and now business manager, Jordan Scott, spotted the potential and the two are working together to grow a company that offers a special and unique product.

Conways Origami started on an informal footing in May 2009 as Matt promoted his hobby in local pubs. The positive feedback turned into early commissions for birthday bouquets and romantic gestures. After researching the market, Matt and Jordan realised this hobby could be turned into a viable business. As Jordan explains:

"Matt has to balance his passion for origami with working as a bar manager in his local pub. As his free time is limited I approached him offering my services as a graphic designer and creative director. In essence I assume the role of business manager and he is the manufacturer. I was able to produce the brand and the website, which I invested in for no charge to the business in order to get the ball rolling. This partnership will naturally give us a competitive edge in the early stages as I intend to design and produce all our marketing materials so we can devote funds saved to other parts of the business."

Matt and Jordan work from separate home offices but meet every day to discuss commissions and promotion. The plan is to secure contracts from luxury brands, elite weddings and corporate events but they know it's one step at a time. They are promoting themselves locally through the press and by placing flowers on display in local restaurants and pubs, complete with a fistful of business cards for people to take away.

TIP

"Ensure you're entering into something for which you have a passion and research the market."

"We have also made contact with Japanese companies with a UK presence and offered branded origami pieces for events, seminars, exhibitions or as a memorable promotional item. We are in contact with the top three Japanese national chain restaurants and initial negotiations are very exciting. Ideally we'd like to take on origami apprentices so Matt and I could focus on sales and product development. We've had a great start and are looking forward to what happens next!"

Give up the day job?

"Yes," said Matt. "I didn't make the important decision to invest limited spare time and money into a venture which I didn't believe could bloom (pardon the pun). One has to be realistic, though. I started with next to no cash and just my skill but was fortunate enough to team up with Jordan who also recognised the potential. With our current strategy going to plan I should be going full-time in the business within 1 year of its inception.

• www.conwaysorigami.com

18 Picture artist

Name: Kelly Brett
Company name: PiddleyPix.com
Day job: Admin officer for a children's centre

After the birth of her first child, Kelly Brett started to draw pictures for the nursery wall. Both Kelly and her husband love being creative so she suggested that they make some more and try to sell them.

"That spurred on my hubby's enthusiasm and our shared passion grew into Piddley Pix! I suggested it as a business in March 2009 and we started the very next month."

Both Kelly and her husband now draw, inspired by their children and nephews.

"They are our inspiration; things they like, things they do or say. Ideas pop into my head during the working day and there are the other typical sources such as books, movies and TV. We just love doing what we do."

The pictures are sold online via the Piddley Pix site and offline by attending baby fairs and local events. Within a short time Kelly made some firm relationships; a local independent retailer is stocking the products and there are flyers going out via local companies who are happy for their clients to hear about this bright new venture. Kelly is expanding the range to include new sizes and frames and is taking orders for bespoke pictures and personalised items.

"My husband is self-employed and works from home, which means that everything we do is centred around the family home. My 9-5 job is an essential part of our life for now, but our passion is for our family business."

The time between arriving home from work and the children's bedtime is family time and after that Piddley Pix work gets done – products are developed, orders are processed and emails dealt with.

"The combination of Piddley Pix and our domestic life is what makes us who we are. We are a close family – we keep each other balanced, and this leads to a healthy environment in our work and our home!"

Give up the day job?
"That would be the ideal. I'd love to be working from home to watch the children bloom. Piddley Pix was born from a hobby, and what would be better than having a full-time job getting paid to do my hobby – that would be fantastic!"

- www.piddleypix.com
- twitter.com/piddleypix

19 Furniture maker

Name: James Fletcher and Sharon Phillips
Company name: Unique Wild Wood Furniture
Day job: James is a general builder and Sharon is a painter and decorator

In their spare time Sharon and Fletch (as James is known) work together to produce beautifully handcrafted coffee tables and works of art made from natural timber.

The couple have been running the business for 2 years and came to rely on the income as the 2008-09 recession had a negative impact on their work, with house building projects drying up. Skills gained through years of working in construction meant Fletch developed his passion for carpentry.

Pieces of furniture are custom-made and produced from hand-picked timber. No matter how unusual the customer's request, the company is able to produce a unique piece that meets requirements.

The couple promote the business online and are now looking for a retail outlet. Roles are divided, with Fletch being hands-on with the craftsmanship and Sharon in control of the admin and business development.

Give up the day job?

"We would love to spend all our time working on the furniture. However, in this current climate we need our full-time jobs."

- www.uniquewildwoodfurniture.co.uk
- twitter.com/uniquewildwood

Jewellery designer

20

Name: Anne Clark
Company name: Angel Eden
Day job: Civil servant

Anne Clark started making jewellery in the lead-up to her daughter's wedding several years ago. Her work began with bending silver wire and adding Swarovski crystals. After the wedding Anne attended an evening class to learn how to make silver jewellery and solder. After this tuition she was able to make more ornate pieces such as English country cottages, garden utensils and cupcakes.

"I became interested in recycling and using vintage items within my jewellery. In an antique shop I found some old glass drops from chandeliers and experimented with silver wire and crystals to give the drops a new lease of life. I also make brooches from recycled fabric, adding old buttons, lace and charms."

Anne makes her fine pieces whilst also working 9 to 5 4 days a week and spending 1 day a week helping her daughter who has three young children. "Saturday is usually spent out and about with my husband and sometimes the grandchildren. Sunday morning we go to church and the rest of the day I spend on the business. I work in the kitchen to make the jewellery or in the dining room if working on the computer. I'm still able to watch the television with my husband and ask his advice on what I'm doing."

Anne has continued to upgrade her website with "each one getting a bit more useful" and her current site offers the ability to buy online. She networks online and is becoming known in all the right places.

"I am learning how to use Photoshop to improve the quality of my photographs. I try to write a blog at least twice a month and if I find interesting blogs written by others, I leave comments. I'm a member of sites I find interesting, such as Enterprise Nation, All About You and UK Handmade. I join in the forums and post comments on how to make jewellery.

"I have uploaded my profile on several sites such as the Association for Contemporary Jewellery, Creative Industries Network, WIRE and Arts Derbyshire and have also posted details on Gumtree and FreeIndex. I have attended workshops to learn how to improve my website and get it noticed. I network through Twitter and spend a few minutes each day on this. I am also on Facebook but need to spend some time getting to grips with the best way to use it."

Anne meets customers face-to-face by selling jewellery at local festivals and craft fairs, delivering demonstrations in local shops, talking to pupils in schools and running workshops from home. She's one busy lady!

Give up the day job?
"I'm due to retire from my day job in the next few months and will then have more daytime hours to spend on my business. I'll also be able to have a social life again!"

- www.angeleden.co.uk

- All About You: www.allaboutyou.com
- Arts Derbyshire: www.artsderbyshire.org.uk
- Association for Contemporary Jewellery: www.acj.org.uk
- Creative Industries Network: www.creative-cin.co.uk (Derbyshire-focused but similar networks exist in other regions of the UK)
- FreeIndex: www.freeindex.co.uk @freeindex
- Gumtree: www.gumtree.com @uk_gumtree
- Holts Academy of Jewellery: www.holtsacademy.com
- UK Handmade: www.ukhandmade.co.uk @ukhandmade
- WIRE: www.wireuk.org @wireuk

Selling jewellery online: Advice from *The Good Web Guide*

Keep it simple

A clean white interface and simple layout and design, will make it easy for visitors to view and buy your jewellery. Resist the urge to use a dark background, which makes it difficult to see photos or read text.

Images tell a thousand words

Professionally taken photos not only let customers see for themselves what they're buying, but will encourage the press to write about and use images of your jewellery.

Be transparent

By having a clear returns policy, visitors will feel more comfortable about buying online. Likewise, give clear information about each piece of jewellery and tell the customer about yourself: people like to know what and from whom they are buying.

- www.thegoodwebguide.com
- @thegoodwebguide

21 Footwear designer

Name: Janan Leo
Company name: CocoRose London
Day job: New product development manager for a rail company

Janan Leo created the concept for CocoRose London, a brand of innovative, foldable ballerina pumps, in early 2007. She set to work on product development and branding and the company officially launched in May 2008.

Janan knew that to make the business work (and to maintain a high standard of quality in her day job) she had to outsource as much as possible and brush up on her time management and organisation skills. Activities such as PR and website design were contracted out to other professionals, giving Janan the time to focus on meeting new contacts and building the business.

"I try to network as much as I can through business events, friends, websites, social media sites, etc. I always carry some of our postcards. The other day I walked past a lady changing into heels from her flip-flops and had to stop and introduce myself. It turns out she is the marketing manager for a fantastic organisation and we're now working together. Yes, sometimes it takes a bit of courage but the worst thing is not trying."

Janan works with her PR consultant to come up with promotional campaigns to coincide with new range

TIP

"If possible, involve your partner. You'll end up spending more time together and talking shop is more fun!

"Extract enjoyment from the ordinary or what may be perceived as normal routine because that is your free time; like walking or going food shopping."

launches and she started a monthly newsletter which is sent to customers, informing them of products, events, competitions and prizes.

"What's so fantastic about modern technology is the ability to have your online shop open 24/7. Although I have a day job, it doesn't mean my business has to stop working!"

LINKS

For identifying marketing, PR and other business professionals

- Business Smiths: Expert support for small businesses www.businesssmiths.co.uk
- Direct Marketing Line: An outsourced marketing service managed on your behalf www.directmarketingline.com
- PeoplePerHour: Find the best deal on a rated freelancer www.peopleperhour.com @peopleperhour
- Wooshii: Source creative talent to work on your viral advertising and marketing www.wooshii.com @wooshii

Most of the company's online sales come from the UK but, with a growing reputation, orders are being picked up from South Africa, Hong Kong and Hawaii. Janan sells her shoes to boutiques in Japan and Beirut and recently secured a deal to sell her collections to a fashion distributor in Milan. Not bad for a business that's run in a few spare hours!

"Setting up and developing a business whilst being in full-time employment and also ensuring time for myself, partner and friends is tough but this is life, it's busy and that's when it's exciting!"

Give up the day job?
"I consider myself very lucky. I work for a great company and am part of an amazing brand. I really enjoy the role I have and what we achieve as a team. I've been very open and honest with them about CocoRose and they fully support my entrepreneurial flair! At some point, yes, I would love to dedicate more time to CocoRose and ultimately, that is what I'm working towards."

- www.cocoroselondon.com
- twitter.com/cocoroselondon

Janan Leo was the Enterprise Nation 2009 Home Business of the Year

For tips on effective outsourcing, see page 209.

22 Clothing producer

Name: Sarah and Andy Goodall
Company name: inkydeep
Day job: Both local government, Andy in IT and Sarah in democratic services

After short careers in the Royal Navy, Sarah and Andy Goodall found themselves working in London, Andy as an IT systems engineer and Sarah as director of a marketing company. It was during this time that the couple watched the film *Big Wednesday* and their interest in surfing was sparked.

"We travelled to Newquay for a surf lesson. Little did we know what a profound impact this would have on our lives. In early 1994 we made tentative steps to set up a surf shop in Southend but the costs scared us off. In 1995 we sold our house in Essex, parked our careers and went travelling round the world for 6 months. Reluctant to return to London we settled in laid back Newquay on Cornwall's beautiful north coast."

Andy and Sarah continued to toy with the idea of starting a surf-clothing business but it wasn't until 2005 that they picked up the pace. Having noticed in other crowded sectors of retail that there was a market for organic, small and honest brands, they felt this could be the point of difference in their own range of surfing t-shirts. They use graphic designers to design the t-shirts and specialist suppliers to produce them.

"Surprisingly there still aren't a lot of organic t-shirt suppliers around. We must have looked at every one on the market and in the end found a great product we are proud to offer our customers. We've worked closely with a design agency on the graphics but we also actively encourage people to submit designs to us for consideration."

Andy and Sarah are now committed to developing the brand and increasing online sales. Once the brand is better established they hope to sell wholesale, seeing the opportunity of many independent surf shops who are not tied into selling a particular label.

Give up the day job?

"Definitely! We would see things getting to where the business could allow one of us to give up their full-time job."

(This causes some interesting chats about who it would be – Andy sees it as an opportunity to surf more and Sarah indicates that this is a risk and therefore it shouldn't be Andy!)

* www.inkydeep.com

For more information on creating a home on the web, see page 197.

TIP

Find your point of difference in the market.

"*As soon as you have a name for your business, secure your domain name, in particular .com and .co.uk. If the name is unique, short and memorable there is more chance that your customers will remember your web address.*
"*If your site is going to be designed and created by a design agency write a requirement specification and ensure this document is used to manage the project. The National B2B Centre has useful resources to help plan your website.*"

LINKS

* National B2B Centre: www.nb2bc.co.uk

Domain registration and web hosting companies

* 123-reg www.123-reg.co.uk
* Low Cost Names: www.lowcostnames.co.uk
* Go Daddy: www.godaddy.com
* Heart Internet: www.heartinternet.co.uk

23 Baby wear supplier

Name: Cheryl Kelly
Company name: Precious Nappies
Day job: Medical sales manager

With a new baby in tow, Cheryl Kelly started her business on 1 January 2009. She's growing the business whilst still working 3 days a week for a medical company.

"I had the idea after my second child was born and whilst on maternity leave decided to develop my plans into a business. When I was looking at using cloth nappies for my new baby, the information available was so confusing and coming from a sales background I knew that if the information on offer wasn't clear customers would walk away. I always wanted my own business and had been searching for the right idea for years but for some reason this just seemed right. The more I found out, the more passionate I became about setting up!"

Cheryl started by looking for a European manufacturer to make cloth nappies to a standard she was happy with. It was also important that the company shared the same ethical and legal policies as the UK and the product could be land-shipped to reduce the impact on the environment. Cheryl chose a company in Turkey and is keeping them busy.

Having worked in sales for the past 9 years, Cheryl is applying her skills to increase orders. She attends events, and is working closely with local midwives, taking her products to their antenatal and parentcraft classes. She is attending pregnancy yoga and exercise classes and has also signed up to a number of local baby exhibitions and shows.

"Knowing I have started this from scratch and will only get out as much as I am willing to put in is such a huge motivator for me!"

Cheryl has a business plan which is regularly reviewed and uses a checklist to ensure she's meeting and achieving her goals. She has been open with her employers from the start about the business.

"I have been working 9 to 5 and 5 to midnight for the past few months and achieved an awful lot in a short space of time, but I couldn't do it without the support of my family. We discussed how the business and working a day job was going to affect our family dynamics and have committed to making it work. The children know their roles and my husband is incredibly supportive."

Give up the day job?
"I'm in a difficult position because I love my day job as well as enjoying the business. Being a medical rep it's not a 9-5 job and you do end up bringing work home with you, so I have to plan my evenings and days off very carefully to ensure I'm committed to both jobs. It will probably stay this way for a while!"

*   www.preciousnappies.co.uk

Name: Daniel Chapman and Carly Clarke
Company name: Twinkly Babies
Day job: Daniel is an IT manager and Carly is a mum

Daniel Chapman took a week off work in September 2009 to launch an online boutique for baby products, along with his partner Carly, who is a full-time mum.

"Carly fits in the work when our son is napping or at playgroup. We both have laptops with wireless internet so our home/work environment is very flexible. We have to-do lists which help us decide what work to tackle next. We all get together for dinner and have family time until 7pm when our son goes to bed and then we really knuckle down and work."

The couple enjoy running the business together and have clear and defined roles, with Daniel managing the accounts and IT functions, whilst Carly takes care of products and customer relations.

The couple makes full use of online advertising methods such as Google AdWords and utilise Amazon Marketplace. They have partnered with other small businesses with similar target markets such as independent midwives, nurseries and baby photographers, and in an effort to keep fit they deliver their leaflets in and around the local area.

The company operates a scheme whereby agents earn up to 25% commission on sales made. To find agents, Twinkly Babies advertises in forums specifically targeting mums on maternity leave or at home and looking to earn income, or people already selling complimentary products. Encouraging their friends to start selling has also worked well.

"We regard our agents more as a part of the Twinkly Babies team and spend a lot of time talking to them about the products and helping them throughout the whole process."

Dan and Carly are also keen adopters of technology. "Our payment terminals and payment processing system is all virtual so we have no physical equipment and no rental charges and can process online, telephone and mail-order card payments. We both have a Blackberry so can respond to emails wherever we are and we use Royal Mail SmartStamp for all of our postage."

Give up the day job?
"Absolutely!" say Daniel. "This is the reason we started the business; to give Carly a salary and for me to eventually be able to leave my full-time job. I love running a business so it's like a hobby to me anyway, but I would love the flexibility and excitement of running the business full time."

* www.twinklybabies.co.uk
* twitter.com/twinklybabies

LINKS

* Baby Expo: For the south and south-east
  www.brightonbabyexpo.co.uk
* The Baby Show: The main event, attracts over 76,000 visitors across three events in Birmingham and London
  www.thebabyshow.co.uk
  @TheBabyShow
* The Scottish Baby Show Scotland's biggest baby event
  www.thebabyshowscotland.com
* Mother and Baby magazine:
  www.askamum.co.uk/motherandbaby
* National Childbirth Trust (NCT) The UK's leading charity for parents
  www.nct.org.uk
* Prima Baby magazine: www.babyexpert.com
* Royal Mail SmartStamp: Print your own postage labels
  www.royalmail.com/smartstamp

24 Toy maker

Name: Lynne Machin
Company name: Cheeky Moo
Day job: Business adviser

The idea for this cheeky 5 to 9 business came about after Lynne Machin received an enquiry from a farm asking for replications of their logo which consisted of five farm animals. After carrying out market research Lynne discovered a gap in the market for quirky farm animal toys and decided to do something about it by launching Cheeky Moo.

"I didn't end up doing the project for the farm but I did start a new business! We have designed, manufactured and are about to retail a set of farmyard toy animals. There's also a short animation of the animals which I'd like to turn into an educational children's TV programme. I realise this is very difficult to do but I'm going to try my best and already have stories planned."

Lynne's vision is to have the animal characters showing children how to be polite and help each other. Aimed at the younger age group, the plan is to offer a show that complements the toys and makes a difference to children's behaviour.

Income is generated from sales of the toys and there's potential to license the characters so they can be used on any products that fit with the theme.

"I went to the licensing show in London and handed out some copies of the animation on DVD. I've also sent it to Nickelodeon and ITV, so you never know."

A sales executive has made contact, offering to sell the toys on a commission basis in the north of England, leaving Lynne to focus on the strategic direction of the business.

"I cannot believe how much I've had to learn from the initial concept to completion, learning about testing and getting prototypes just right. I started in February 2009 and got the first shipment of toys 9 months later. It has been an incredible experience."

Give up the day job?
"Yes. I would like to build the business and brand and possibly take on staff."

• www.cheekymoo.com

25 Children's party organiser

Name: Louise Graham
Company name: Charming Angels
Day job: Teacher

Louise Graham works full time as a teacher, is a mum, and is growing her young business in the bits of spare time she can claim.

"I'm extremely lucky to have a supportive husband and family who help out around the house. I do make sure I book time off to spend with my family; free weekends are treasured as are family days out."

In fact, one of the main reasons Louise started the business was to spend more time with her son.

"Whilst on holiday I realised I wanted to have more control over my working life and most of all be there for my son as he was growing up."

A new business was the result. The company offers jewellery and craft-making parties and, on the back of a growing profile, Louise is taking more and more bookings. The business is being promoted via mums' websites and forums, in entertainers' directories and in local magazines, as well as a feature in *Red* magazine which brought Louise and her parties to the attention of the nation's mums and fellow party organisers.

"To increase profitability my aim now is to set up an agent scheme so more children and their parents can benefit from the Charming Angels service. Due to it being a fairly local service and having to turn down many bookings due to location, I hope to expand and have agents in all the major UK cities."

Louise has designed and develops her own website so when the agent programme launches she will create video demonstrations and host them online as a learning resource.

"In the office most emails are answered once my son is in bed, or I work on the laptop so I'm still in the family room surrounded by toys and with the television blaring. My son loves to get involved in organising the materials for the parties by sorting beads into boxes. He's a very dedicated employee!"

Give up the day job?
"Yes. I would like to go full-time with the business, or even be able to go part-time at my day job. Watch this space!"

• www.charmingangelsparties.co.uk

26 Leisure & entertainment

Name: John Randall
Company name: JV Bouncy Castle Hire
Day job: Student

John Randall is a university student who finds it simple to maintain a healthy balance between his degree and part-time business. During the week he is located in Oxford Brookes for his studies and on a Friday night commutes back to Basingstoke ready for the weekend when business commences.

"This allows me to separate the two areas nicely and means I stay focused on my studies during the week, and focused on the business at weekends. I do get bookings on weekdays so some administration work has to be done in the evenings, however much of the booking system I use is automated so it only takes around 15 minutes a day to complete."

John's business is offering bouncy castle hire for parties and other special occasions. The main promotion happens through the company website which has been built carefully so it is ranked number one on Google search results when customers search for 'bouncy-castle hire' in the area John serves. Other methods include direct marketing via email to existing customers and cold-calling schools to see if they require inflatables for functions.

John has posters displayed on notice boards at most of the community centres in his area and gives out flyers promoting the business, often handing them out to parents when schools are finishing for the day.

"I buy inflatables second-hand and then get them re-furbished to an 'as new' condition. This saves me thousands of pounds in equipment costs. I send Christmas cards that contain a £10 gift voucher to previous customers which encourages repeat bookings and helps to create a better relationship."

The online booking system sends details to John's email account and as a message to his mobile phone. This means he can give a prompt response when customers have an enquiry. There's also a fully automated invoicing system that makes keeping on top of accounts a whole lot easier.

"It provides a professional invoice for my customers and keeps a copy on file. The software is great for analysing when I'm busiest and which of my products are the most popular."

Give up the day job?
"I plan to keep the business going as long as possible. The perfect scenario for me is to either start a 'main' business once I graduate or work for an employer. I'll save the income from my business so I can eventually purchase a home. I have saved half my turnover this year and plan to do the same until I graduate."

• www.bouncycastleshire.co.uk

John was the 2009 Enterprise Nation Young Home Business Owner of the Year.

For links to student enterprise groups and resources, see page 148.

> **TIP**
>
> *"When starting a business, take your time. Don't grow it too quickly or you run the risk of neglecting your studies (or other job).*
>
> *"Join the university's entrepreneurship or business societies, Oxford Entrepreneurs has opened up so many doors for me!"*

27 Musician

Name: Vernon Fuller
Company name: Vernon Fuller
Day job: Financial tutor

Vernon Fuller's love of music began as a child. He became more serious at the age of 16 when starting to learn the guitar and, from there on, jazz was his passion.

"I had started playing in bands as a teenager, then got married, started a family and put more time and energy into my credit management career. I reached a point when I decided that if I wanted to further my music career, I needed to promote myself more widely. I set up a website, had some business cards created, attended jam sessions and recorded CDs with other musicians. I also joined my local business chamber and the Musicians' Union and enlisted on the books of several entertainment agencies."

Vernon performs at music festivals, clubs, corporate events, weddings and parties as a solo musician, and with different bands. He has taught guitar and vocals to groups of students for several years and also now teaches on a one-to-one basis.

"Managing my time is a constant juggling act. The balls mostly stay in the air but I do sometimes drop one. Prioritising the important versus the urgent is usually okay but saying no to some requests (I don't like turning work down) is still difficult."

Basic accounting knowledge from Vernon's credit management background has been useful in ensuring invoices are raised and – importantly – paid! Networking and meeting like-minded people has also helped to get Vernon established as a musician.

"I went to jam sessions to meet as many other musicians as possible and to get my name out there. Working 5 to 9 has kick-started a new and exciting phase in my life."

Give up the day job?
"My plan is to build up sales of gigs, CDs and guitar lessons to contribute towards giving up my day job. I plan to start a new business that is more related to my day job but doing fewer hours, to support my musical activities. I also plan to deliver money management classes and am hoping to develop my voice acting work."

*   www.vernonfuller.co.uk
*   www.myspace.com/vernonsfuller

LINKS

*   British Chambers of Commerce www.britishchambers.org.uk
*   Musicians Union www.musiciansunion.org.uk
*   Registry of Guitar Tutors www.registryofguitartutors.co.uk

28 Magician

Name: Jonathan Dowden
Company name: Jonathan Mark Magic
Day job: Business support adviser

After performing for a number of years, Jonathan Dowden decided to turn his skill into a business. Jonathan Mark Magic appeared like a white rabbit out of a hat in late 2008.

"My interest in magic came from watching my brother, Matthew J Dowden, who is a world renowned magician, and realising there was a great way to satisfy my love of performing and develop a business opportunity at the same time."

From his role as a business adviser there are many skills that easily cross over to the 5 to 9 business; one being an appreciation of corporate events as Jonathan attends a good number of them as a guest. So when he changes roles and performs, he's able to provide the best possible service to clients.

"It is vital that you understand what the client is trying to achieve and adapt the magic and your approach to suit. This often gives me an edge over other magicians and ensures I get plenty of repeat business."

Working closely with people in his day job has also honed Jonathan's communication skills, which helps improve the experience for his magic audiences. His business is now of a size that he's performing on weeknights and is often booked at weekends. Engagements range from weddings, to events in bars, to corporate gatherings for companies like HP, Sony and Npower.

"I enjoy working in all these arenas as they require different routines and give me a good excuse to continually buy (sorry invest...) in new props and material."

Handing out business cards at these events means there's a regular stream of business to keep Jonathan occupied.

Give up the day job?

"No way! I love magic and my day job so there are no plans to give it up. I often speak to people who assume the ultimate aim is to turn the part-time business into a full-time one. Why? You get the best of both worlds by being your own boss outside of 9-5 and taking home a regular salary."

* www.jonathanmarkmagic.co.uk
* twitter.com/jmmagic

TIP
"From a commercial standpoint you would never advise a business to rely on one customer for all their income, yet that is what the majority of employees do from one year to the next. Having a 5 to 9 business at least gives you a bit of a safety net should the worst happen in the day job."

29 Beer producer

Name: Harriet Easton
Company name: The Rushing Dolls Company
Day job: Undergraduate

It was during her gap year that Harriet Easton came up with the idea for a beer for women. Developed specifically to appeal to the female palate, and marketed to a female audience, Harry's Beer was launched in December 2007.

"I spotted a gap in the market, in that quality, lightly brewed ales were only marketed to the male consumer. As I started spending time in bars I realised there could be a market opening for a beer designed and, more importantly, packaged for female consumers."

Without knowing anything about the brewing industry, Harriet turned to the Campaign for Real Ale (CAMRA) for information and advice. At both a local and national level, the organisation happily shared its knowledge and expertise. Harriet was invited to events all over the country so she could see first-hand how brewers, sellers and consumers came together. The very first pint of Harry's Beer was drawn by CAMRA's UK chair, Paula Waters!

"I was bowled over with support given by CAMRA. They were so generous with their time and patient with a girl learning about the world of real ale. I also realised I couldn't possibly gain all the knowledge I needed to set up a new business single-handedly so I structured my business to bring in industry expertise in exchange for a shareholding. The Rushing Dolls Company now boasts highly experienced professionals skilled in business strategy, marketing, design, branding and PR."

The business has been co-financed by Harriet's own earnings during her gap year, with further investment from the company's strategic director and her mum.

"My mum sits on the board and is a constant source of inspiration as well as hands-on management whilst I complete my degree."

The company has been promoted through personal appearances at events and beer forums and through broadcast opportunities. During term time Harriet has attended promotional events near where she studies and, during the holidays, meets with fellow directors. The future holds exciting plans for a new sales campaign focused on niche outlets and the 'on-trade' as well as developing the retail sales channels that have been so successful to date.

Give up the day job?
"I'm not giving up my studies! After I graduate I plan to work full time and to also spend more time on the business. The most powerful thing for me has been the experience I've gained which I know will really help when I enter the world of full-time work."

* www.rushingdolls.com

30 Events organiser

Name: Kane Towning
Company name: AIM Events Ltd
Day job: Former undergraduate

Kane Towning started AIM Events Ltd in January 2009 but he was operating long before this, promoting nightclub events and DJing. In fact, he worked full-time throughout his 3 years of studying; attending lectures by day, and promoting club events by night.

"My degree was in entertainment management. I chose this course as it didn't pigeonhole my studies into one area. The entertainment industry is so broad and varied and the course allowed me to learn about many areas of the industry."

The company predominantly promotes clubbing events but is also involved in others such as boxing bouts, product promotion and youth work. There's a strong portfolio of nights out under the AIM Clubbing brand, which range from large-scale, 3000+ people nightclub events to small, unique underground nights. The three founders of the company (Kane plus partners Daniel Bond and Alex Simmons) are continually expanding and taking on more nights around the UK. They've also just completed their first overseas event.

With all this activity underway, it's a wonder Kane had time left over for study.

"It was difficult! There were many times I considered quitting my studies and if it had not had been for my excellent tutor I may not have carried on. It was difficult and frustrating throughout my years of university as I really wanted to gain a degree and study to the best of my ability, but I also wanted to fulfil my dream of owning my own business and doing something I'm so passionate about. I wasn't your typical student, going out every night, not having that much to do, and always being skint. That has never appealed to me!"

When he wasn't attending lectures and tutorials, Kane was in the office working and when he should have been at uni, Kane was still in the office working! But he planned his time well and after a few all-night sessions in the library, made it through and left with a degree and a successful business.

"I came out with the degree I deserved in terms of the work I put in, but on the other hand, for the knowledge I had through my work experience and own ventures, I should have got a first!"

Give up the day job?
Having graduated, Kane is now a full-time director of AIM Events Ltd.

• www.aimclubbing.co.uk

TIP

"There's nothing better than experience. So many people think getting a degree is the key to success in life. They don't realise that you can't read in a book what the big wide world is actually like."

31 Party planner

Name: Mandy Key
Company name: Jamie at Home
Day job: Head of Service Improvement for NHS Community Services

Mandy Key is responsible for developing concepts to support community services in the East Riding of Yorkshire. She advises clinicians and management teams and is an expert on project and programme management. After this day job ends Mandy changes into her role as a Jamie at Home consultant.

"I was attracted to the Jamie at Home opportunity as it was a new and exciting business venture, and of course it was a chance to work in partnership with Jamie himself. There was the added benefit of a strong brand and fabulous designer-led products. I had previous direct-selling experience and saw this as an exciting opportunity."

Mandy signed up as a consultant in April 2009 and has been building sales (and the size of her team of consultants) by promoting parties to her wide-ranging network of contacts.

"I come across a lot of people in my everyday life so have a great platform from which to share my business opportunity. Over the past 20 years I've always held 2 jobs, my full-time day job plus an evening/weekend job. These have included: promotion girl for the local radio station, an exercise to music teacher, diet instructor for Rosemary Conley and a direct-sales consultant. As you can appreciate, my contacts database is, by now, pretty extensive!"

Mandy also advertises to promote her Jamie at Home business on notice boards (in local shops, post office windows, business notice boards, leaflet drops), makes the most of Facebook and regularly invites friends and family round to her house to socialise and be updated on business news.

"This keeps my friends and family informed and gives them an opportunity to buy from my shop at the same time."

With so much to fit in to each day, Mandy is a big believer in practising effective time management and getting her priorities right.

"I use a time-management tool developed by Franklin Covey where you populate your diary with the rocks in your life (loved ones), followed by your pebbles (work) – this should give you a work/family life balance. Then the sand (any additional activities) filters through the gaps."

Give up the day job?
"I enjoy both roles and they really do complement each other. I've recently finished a Masters degree to support my day job and am looking forward to the opportunities this may bring. I also love my business as it's the perfect way to meet people, be my own boss and earn extra money on the way. Both play a very important but different part in my life and I'd like to keep it that way."

• www.jamieathome.com

Name: Terri Rhind
Company name: My Secret Kitchen
Day job: PA/office manager to surveyor

Terri Rhind signed up with My Secret Kitchen, a nationwide food and drink-tasting company, in July 2008, after attending a tasting party.

"I loved the concept of having the products explained to me and being given all the recipe ideas so people really had the opportunity to create different meals from so few products."

Terri started by hosting tastings at her home. This led to bookings in friends' homes, and she now has bookings at strangers' homes as well as appearing at craft fairs and events.

"I promote my business verbally through networking with others in the similar field of party plan. I have great backup from my upline leader and head office with training updates and consultant newsletters."

Give up the day job?
"My aim is to comfortably run My Secret Kitchen alongside my 9 to 5 job for the next 1-2 years, eventually building a team that will enable me to run the company full time."

* www.mysecretkitchen.co.uk

See page 156 for more party plan and home business franchise opportunities.

Mystery shopper

32

Name: Rob Russell
Company name: IMS
Day job: Property management

By day Rob Russell manages properties (his own and on behalf of others) and in his spare time carries out work as a mystery shopper for field marketing agency, IMS.

"The IMS work can be very varied. It is mainly merchandising-based; we visit supermarkets in our area and help set up a promotion or just assist in making sure the store is in a position to maximise sales of the products on promotion. Other work can involve mystery shopping. This may take the form, for example, of visits to mobile phone companies to assess the standards of their customer service."

Working for field marketing agencies is flexible and depends on the campaign. Rob generally allocates 15-18 hours each week to work on IMS and other merchandising company projects, with mystery shopping reports taking anything from 2 to 30 minutes each to complete.

One of the reasons Rob is such a skilled mystery shopper is because he was frequently mystery shopped himself when he was running a garage!

"As we were actively shopped on a regular basis I know what is expected when carrying out these activities myself. For merchandising work it's vitally important you know how to talk to the store staff. You can really improve your in-store results if you are polite and get on the right side of the staff. Building up a good relationship is important, especially if visiting these stores regularly."

Due to the variance of the amount of work on offer, Rob considers his mystery shopping activity as supporting daytime income, as opposed to replacing it.

"Some weeks I may get more work than I can handle and other weeks very little at all. It's for this reason I wouldn't recommend that anyone rely on field marketing as a full-time business but it's perfect for anyone wanting to earn extra income in their spare time."

Give up the day job?
"I'm happy with the mix and variety I have. With it comes great flexibility, giving me time to work on the property lettings, IMS projects and take care of my young daughter. I've got the perfect set-up and want to keep it this way!"

- www.ukims.co.uk

Image consultant

Name: Tracy O'Toole
Company name: Chrysalis Image
Day job: Senior financial consultant for Nationwide Building Society

After studying colour analysis, make-up and womens' and mens' styling, Tracy O'Toole started her image consultancy business to turn the training into turnover. As well as running the business, Tracy works part-time, has two young children and is a former director of membership for the International Federation of Image Consultants.

"I have found that my day-job skills compliment my image consultations. I ask lots of questions to find out what my client is looking for, their preferences, experiences, likes and dislikes, and then apply this information, along with my knowledge and expertise, to present recommendations. These principles can be applied to providing advice, whether financial or colour and styling!"

The most popular service is women's evenings; a 2-hour session tailored to the needs of attendees - for example, fashion trends for the season, wardrobe management and principles of colour.

"I look at other consultants' websites to see what service they offer and to try and make sure my fees are in line."

Tracy has developed the business single-handedly and even though she hasn't involved friends and family, they do show support by providing ad hoc childcare and emotional encouragement which Tracy finds invaluable.

Little advertising has been required as Tracy relies so heavily on word of mouth and referrals. She's keen to make sure she can manage her time well so is hesitant to advertise in case it leads to a rush of bookings that simply can't be delivered.

Give up the day job?

"I would absolutely love to pursue Chrysalis Image on a full-time basis, but at the moment I need the consistent income and benefits provided by my employer. This also has the advantage of not having to put pressure on my business to achieve a specific level of income every month. I think it's likely I will be looking to build the business further once both of my children are at school."

- www.chrysalisimage.com

LINKS

- Association of Image Consultants International www.aici.org
- International Federation of Image Consultants www.tfic.org.uk

Personal development practitioner

34

Name: Nicola Kelsall
Company name: Spiralling
Day job: Teacher

Nottinghamshire-based Nicola Kelsall is a full-time teacher and her school's head of philosophy. Outside of work, she runs Spiralling with her husband Tom (who also works full-time). Spiralling sells meditation CDs and other aids (incense, artefacts, statues, etc) and instruments (drums, flutes, gongs and percussion) as well as offering sound therapy treatments.

Nicola says working 5 to 9 has helped the couple build the business slowly and pay the bills at the same time.

"For instance, it paid for us to have the CDs professionally recorded and allowed us to launch the collection. We've been able to pay to develop the business without having to borrow any money. It has also allowed us the space to learn our skills – Tom makes the flutes we sell, and he has been able to perfect the craft without the pressure of having to make money from them immediately."

Nicola has also been able to perfect her drum-making skills, and take the time to become properly qualified as a sound therapist. When she broke her wrist, it meant there was still an income even though Nicola couldn't make drums or perform therapy for 3 months.

TIP

"Be organised, set yourself targets and goals for a day, a week etc, but schedule in time for a rest!"

Although Spiralling is not the most obvious extension of Nicola's day job, one does inspire the other:

"As a teacher, I see current ideas about dealing with certain conditions within school, and that has allowed us to look at pursuing new avenues in the business. Working the day job and building the business is a perfect mix."

Give up the day job?

"I am hoping in the future to have built two businesses; offering mantra therapy and selling my CDs through Spiralling, and selling children's books with Barefoot Books. Expanding both businesses will allow me to eventually leave teaching."

• www.spiralling.co.uk

Fitness adviser

35

Name: Julie Mitchell-Mehta
Company name: Fitnag.com
Day job: Founder of Début Marketing

Not content with being the boss of one business, Julie Mitchell-Mehta decided to set up another in her spare time! By day she runs Début Marketing, a consultancy which helps small businesses with their marketing communications, and by night she runs fitnag.com, which offers motivational emails and diet and fitness advice on a weekly basis for people who want encouragement to get or keep fit.

For 10 years Julie had a secret dream of becoming a personal trainer. Lack of time and money has prevented it being realised, but having recently taken up running, she found herself advising a number of friends on how to get started and nagging them to keep it up. Julie decided that providing online advice and motivation was a step towards her goal and something she'd enjoy doing without having to leave the house at the kids' bedtime. Julie's skills from her day job are certainly coming in handy.

"My marketing skills have been helpful in many ways – writing my business plan, registering domain names, designing and writing my website and knowing where to go for help. I will also draw on those skills when doing PR and advertising for the launch."

TIP

"Be very organised. Keep a note of what needs to be done in each business so you don't miss any deadlines."

Julie initially plans to promote fitnag.com online using Twitter, Facebook and GoogleAds, as well as through online forums and networks. She is tapping into the expertise of a number of friends who provide diet, nutrition, fitness and injury advice, and with the marketing company providing work on a project basis, Julie feels this helps with her time management.

"My marketing business has ups and downs depending on when projects come in. I am either very busy or pretty quiet so I can use the quiet spells to work on fitnag.com. My marketing clients come first, and when they have a project for me, it is my priority but once I have finished my marketing work then I spend time on fitnag.com. In the long run I see fitnag.com providing a steady trickle of work which will take up a regular number of hours each week and my marketing business continuing to provide bursts of work."

Give up the day job?
"I would like fitnag to bring in a regular income so it reduces the pressure to find new marketing business, but I definitely want to keep Début Marketing going. I have a lot of marketing knowledge, I am a chartered marketer and still enjoy marketing – using those skills to set up and promote my own business gives me additional experience which can only benefit my marketing clients."

- www.fitnag.com
- twitter.com/fitnag

Personal trainer

36

Name: Andy Hawkswell
Company name: Sweat Personal Training
Day job: Manager of a chain of gyms

Andy Hawkswell is in the fortunate position of working flexible hours in his day job of managing 3 gyms in the Harrogate area. He can work around this job and offer a quality service to clients of his part-time business, Sweat Personal Training, which launched in January 2006. Andy trains clients whenever they require sessions and fits his management role around his personal training work.

"My work does help me develop Sweat as I see and speak to my target market every day. As I am the gyms' manager I need to be up-to-date with all the latest industry trends and exercise techniques so work funds a lot of my training and continuous professional development."

Andy promotes Sweat PT with business cards and flyers in the gyms he manages and has a website and Facebook page. He advertises on free online listings such as Yell.com and has the Sweat logo and contact details on his car.

"The car has been a fantastic way of attracting attention. It is probably my most successful method of advertising to date."

TIP

"Plan your business carefully and ensure you know who your target market is, which will in turn influence where and how you advertise."

LINKS

Premier Training International
premierglobal.co.uk

The company also sponsors local events such as the Harrogate 10k road race, so Andy gets his flyers and promotional material in the goodie bags.

"I have tried advertising in industry magazines, newspapers, shops and sports clubs but they never seem that successful. I also have been on Google AdWords but without any success. This has been a learning curve for me, so now I try to be more specific with my advertising and marketing."

Give up the day job?

My plan is to resign from my employment and be self-employed on a full-time basis within the next 12 months.

* www.sweatpersonaltraining.co.uk

Lifestyle adviser

37

Name: Haoming Yau
Company name: Promise Aid
Day job: Project officer for community enterprise consultancy

Haoming Yau did not start his 5 to 9 venture to make money; he started it as a sideline activity that would help people make positive lifestyle choices. In turn it's helped him to change his own lifestyle in the form of a new job.

"There was no eureka moment that comes with many start-ups – I just had a goal that I wanted to create something that would make a difference so came up with a number of ideas that I kept developing. The concept for Promise Aid was born after doing a lot of research, setting aside time to be creative and trying to learn as much as possible about web start-ups."

The site is an online portal that helps people make and keep positive lifestyle promises, such as giving up smoking, losing weight, learning something new or getting out of debt. The website lets users make a commitment to action, track their progress, connect with fellow promisers, watch inspiring videos, get related news and share useful resources. Yau intends to generate revenue from the site through advertising as traffic grows.

TIP

> *"Make sure you spend time with your family and friends and relax. Don't neglect other areas of your life such as health and relationships. It's great if you've got a day job or business that you are passionate about but remember there is more to life than work."*

"It's early days yet so the website doesn't take any revenue but the costs to keep it running are not high. The only fixed cost I have at the moment is the hosting. All other costs are associated with improving the website and getting more visitors. All the features are free. The site has the potential to make revenue through online advertising in a variety of forms such as Google AdSense, affiliates, advertising partnerships and newsletter sponsorships."

Promise Aid will be able to offer targeted marketing opportunities as promises can be matched with relevant products and services. Yau has also secured work by helping people with their own websites and has made money from selling a website domain, but his priority is to focus on creating something that brings value to users. He sees Promise Aid as a social enterprise and wants it to be something that genuinely helps people.

Give up the day job?

"I did work part-time for a few months to spend more hours on Promise Aid but soon realised that having a full-time job lets me save the money I need to invest in the business. Pursuing a not-for-profit venture can really boost your career prospects and opens up opportunities. I have had job offers because of my work on Promise Aid. I now work as a project officer for a community enterprise consultancy which I'm finding rewarding, so I am happy to keep both my job and the business going."

*   www.promiseaid.com

LINKS

- Social Enterprise Mark: A mark that tells customers you trade as a social enterprise - www.socialenterprisemark.co.uk
- Social Enterprise Awards: An awards programme dedicated to social enterprises - www.socialenterpriseawards.org.uk
- Social Enterprise Coalition: Online resource for social enterprises, including a map of regional social enterprise bodies - www.socialenterprise.org.uk
- UnLtd: Charity supporting social entrepreneurs - www.unltd.org.uk

38 Homestager

Name: Semona Glace
Company name: Home Stagers
Day job: Personal Assistant

Homestaging was practically invented in the UK by the highly entrepreneurial Tina Jesson who founded Home Stagers to offer others an opportunity to set up their own business, advising clients on how to sell their home in the most effective way. Someone who has taken the training and is about to step into the world of working 5 to 9 is Semona Glace, who is currently a PA by day and student by night, soon to be homestager by night.

"Homestaging involves de-personalising properties before putting them up for sale. Staging creates an environment that will lead a buyer's eye to the home's attractive features, while minimising its flaws. I'm in the process of completing the Home Stagers home study course, and study at the weekends and in the evenings. I will continue this pattern when I start my own business."

Once Semona has graduated she will be her own boss, operating in London and the surrounding counties. She will be responsible for marketing and promoting the business, which will involve approaching estate agents and working on direct marketing with local flyer campaigns. She will retain a connection with Home Stagers who provide ongoing training and support.

Semona has big plans – as does Tina Jesson – who is re-launching the British Academy of Home Stagers and adding a new e-learning institute which will allow flexibility for students from around the world. They will be able to take programmes and exams online. The programmes include staging, show homes, furniture rental and training on business start-up, growth and strategic development for students wanting to make a full-time career/business out of staging.

Home Stagers offers a training opportunity that will furnish you with the skills and set you free to develop the business, which is just what Semona is about to do.

Give up the day job?
"Yes, definitely. I want to build sales so I can dedicate myself fully to the business as soon as possible."

LINKS

- British Academy of Homestagers www.britishacademyofhomestagers.com
- Home Stagers www.homestagers.co.uk

39 Photographer

Name: Derek Houghton
Company name: Houghton Images
Day job: Document management operations manager

Derek Houghton has enjoyed photography since he was a child. In April 2009 he decided to turn his photographic passion into a living and registered as a freelance photographer offering digital imaging services.

"The business can be very varied, from fine art photography to scanning and restoring old prints, sports or music events to portraits and maintaining websites. The options are wide and I am looking to find a niche in the market specialising in sports, music and small business."

Derek has over 20 years' management experience and has found this useful in establishing his own venture. Images are sold online through Derek's own website and via sales to the big image stock sites as well as in various local outlets including a gallery in Ironbridge.

Plans for the next 12 months include developing a mobile facility for studio photography and portraits and attending events such as sport matches where Derek will shoot and sell on-site. Investment has been made in lighting, printing and backdrop equipment.

"In the first year building contacts was the key element to my initial growth, and I'm now building on my working relationships in order to expand the business."

Marketing has been successful on the back of membership of a home business hub facility in Shropshire called Enterprise HQ, and Derek now has a small office/gallery/studio space within the facility.

"Networking with other photographers and local businesses has been a fantastic way to promote myself. Web-based technology like Twitter and MySpace are giving me options to pursue; however, there is nothing better than getting out there and meeting people."

"Make a plan and stick to it but always look out for opportunities. Aim high and persevere."

Give up the day job?
"Once the income from photography overtakes the income from the day job then I will seriously consider it. It's currently my retirement plan and I hope to be doing it for a very long time."

- www.shropshire-images.com
- twitter.com/derekhoughton

LINKS

- The Association of Photographers
  www.the-aop.org
- Flickr.com
  Useful for displaying photographic portfolio
  www.flickr.com @flickr

Image libraries
- Alamy www.alamy.com
- Fotolia www.fotolia.com
- fotoLibra www.fotolibra.com
- Getty Images www.gettyimages.com
- iStockphoto www.istockphoto.com

Home business hub facilities

Hub facilities are springing up fast in villages, market towns and cities. These 'third spaces' offer a place of work that's outside the home, and a meeting location that's more professional than the local coffee shop. Access these facilities to hot desk when you want to feel the buzz of human activity or to present yourself to clients.

Here are just a few from across the UK. To locate the hub facility that's closest to you, visit www.enterprisenation.com and click on the third spaces map.

Bedfordshire	Funkbunk	www.funkbunk.com
Birmingham Bristol London Manchester	eOffice	www.eoffice.net
Bristol London	The Hub	www.the-hub.net
Bristol	Watershed	www.watershed.co.uk
Huddersfield	Huddersfield Media Centre	www.the-media-centre.co.uk
Leicester	Leicester Creative Business Depot	www.lcbdepot.co.uk
North East	Space on Tap	www.spaceontap.com
Sheffield	Electricworks	www.electric-works.net
Shropshire	Enterprise HQ	www.enterprise-hq.co.uk
Somerset	Forward Space	www.forwardspace.co.uk
Wales	Indycube	www.indycube.biz
Wandsworth	Third Door	www.third-door.com

If you're looking more for the wi-fi enabled coffee shop option, sign up to www.meatspaces.com or check out iPhone application WorkSnug (www.worksnug.com) which connects mobile workers to workspaces across the globe.

Accountant

Name: Emily Coltman
Company name: Home Business Accountant
Day job: Support accountant

In 2009 Emily Coltman launched an accountancy practice aimed at people starting and growing a business from home. In doing so she came to the attention of FreeAgent Central, a company producing online accounting software specifically aimed at freelancers and small businesses. FreeAgent offered Emily a job, she accepted and went from being a full-time business owner to a 5 to 9 business owner. It's a move she feels works well for all concerned.

"My new employer is happy for me to keep my business going in my spare hours, particularly as several of my clients use and love their software! This means I can truly understand the software as I'm experiencing it as an employee and as a user. Other accountants who might be considering using the software with their clients can talk to someone experienced in it and can see it from their side. Everybody wins."

Emily will be putting a cap on the number of clients she deals with as she doesn't want to compromise on the level of service she provides, not only to the clients but also to her employer. To make the arrangement work Emily makes the most of technology so clients and contacts remain informed.

TIP

"Don't overdo it! Make time to be with family and friends too."

"I already use the excellent Moneypenny for answering my calls, and my clients know I will get back to them as quickly as possible. I also use an auto-responder on my email so clients aren't left wondering if I'm ignoring them!"

As for the accountancy aspects of running a 5 to 9 business, Emily advises her clients to notify the tax man even if trading is only part-time. It's important to do this within 3 months of starting to trade to avoid being fined. Emily also suggests that owners carefully consider their business structure as, with limited time available, you don't want to spend it dealing with mountains of paperwork.

Give up the day job?

"No. The day job is a very exciting new challenge and I'm enjoying it."

- www.homebusinessaccountant.co.uk
- twitter.com/homebusacct

For information on your accounting position as a 5 to 9'er, see page 172.

LINKS

- FreeAgent Central www.freeagentcentral.com
- Institute of Chartered Accountants in England & Wales www.icaew.com
- Moneypenny PA www.moneypenny.co.uk @MoneypennyPA

Lawyer

41

Name: Rob Birkett
Company name: Leaving Ltd
Day job: Shipping lawyer

Leavinglaw.com is a community site providing ideas, inspiration, impetus and guidance for lawyers seeking a career change. It was started and is managed by Rob Birkett who is a lawyer by day and entrepreneur by night. Yet Rob claims no credit for coming up with the big idea.

"It was my sister's idea. She was much happier after summoning the courage to leave the world's biggest law firm, and thereafter became a big advocate of being brave enough to do what makes you happy, rather than what you feel you should be doing. We embarked on the project together, but shortly afterwards she had a third child and moved abroad, leaving me with her blessing to continue on my own. I think my brother-in-law's blessing was given at the point I showed my sister the web design quotes!"

Rob does not see the site having any conflict with his day job (working in law yet assisting people in leaving law) as it's an information pool helping people who have already realised law is not for them but are struggling to find a way off the treadmill. One of the most popular sections on the site is 'Alternatives within legal practice', which looks at roles such as public sector law or starting your own law firm. These are options whereby lawyers

TIP

"Keep going! Hang in there with the day job as long as you can make it tenable. Don't burn bridges before you can see which direction things are going. If I'd have stopped working when I first thought of resigning in order to concentrate on leavinglaw, I would be living under a bridge. With a laptop."

get to ply their trade but without the pressures of billing targets and time sheets.

"Many young people enter law with a degree of blind faith, based on the fact they want to be in an established profession, or on advice from their parents, or simply believing it offers things it does not, or no longer does. Law, in particular, can manifest stress and strain so it's only natural this focuses people on what really motivates and interests them. I believe it's not until you reach your thirties that you start to find out who you really are, and that can lead to its own epiphany in terms of your life, career and ambitions."

Rob is following his own ambitions and promoting the site to lawyer friends and colleagues as well as on message boards, forums and social networking sites. Revenue is being generated from online advertising and the content continues to grow.

"The internet enables the compilation of information, available via one site that can be conveniently and surreptitiously accessed from the desk in your office. Otherwise the research for an endeavour such as a career change can be enormous."

Give up the day job?
"Yes, this is my aim. That said, the cathartic experience of having leavinglaw outside of the day job actually lifts my spirits, and that is reflected in the enjoyment of my employment. We'll see how things evolve. It's been really inspirational seeing some of the amazing things people have gone on to do for themselves and I'd still like to be part of that."

- www.leavinglaw.com
- twitter.com/leavinglaw

Translator

Name: Wendy Stott
Company name: Currently freelancing, company not formed
Day job: Resource coordinator for London Underground

Wendy Stott studied French, Russian, Spanish, Japanese and business at university. Her choice of degree reflected a love of languages that started during an exchange visit to France when Wendy was just 13. It was to be the first of many visits, culminating in 5 years spent working in Paris for a leading French law firm. This experience sparked Wendy's interest in translation and, now back in the UK, she is turning her language skills into a way of earning extra income. But money is not the only motivator for this 5 to 9'er.

"I'm starting to think about having children. When I become a mum I'd like to be working in a way that allows me to stay at home with the children yet carry on earning. That's why I'm building up translation work in my spare time – I'm paving the way for what will hopefully become a full-time career."

Wendy's employer is aware of the out-of-hours working arrangement and, as Wendy comments, "my boss knows I do some translation work to top up my income and it doesn't pose a problem".

The plan is to develop relationships with business clients, as opposed to individuals. Wendy knows the work has to be regular and at a rate that pays the bills; business contracts achieve this but ad hoc work for individual private clients does not. Wendy generates work from two main translation sites – Lingo24.com and Language123.com – and has found such sites invaluable in getting her started but she would like to move towards direct and long-term relationships with her clients.

"I started translating just to keep my languages going but it's also meant I'm now building a business so ultimately I'll be able to work for myself."

Wendy is about to invest in a suite of translation software which will make her working life more efficient and later this year a trip to Russia will help brush up her skills. Keeping her French up-to-date isn't a problem as Wendy's partner is French so acts as the perfect teacher and coach. He also works for the London Underground but has no plans to become a 5 to 9'er ... just yet!

Give up the day job?
"I'm not yet close to earning enough to go full-time in the business and I enjoy my day job. The plan is to build up the translation work gradually, and maintain a top service for clients, so when the time comes to have children, I'll have the choice to work from home and be a good mum and business woman!"

- wendystott.language123.com

LINKS

- Language123 www.language123.com
- Lingo24 www.lingo24.com

IT services

43

Name: Ruth Cheesley
Company name: Suffolk Computer Services
Day job: Surveillance and audit data analyst for the NHS

It was through helping friends with their IT troubles that Ruth Cheesley discovered her talent for explaining things in a way that a non-IT person could understand.

"My first venture was Essex Virus Removals. Our university helpdesk was sending students to PC World to get their viruses removed and my friends were being charged a high amount for something which only took a few hours to fix, so I set about helping fellow students by removing viruses and carrying out other IT and computer-related tasks. I didn't start it to make lots of money but to help other students and pay for a few beers at the weekend!"

The business has since grown significantly, mainly through word of mouth and a small amount of networking Ruth did when the business was launched. But this 5 to 9 business and the day job are far from the only things in Ruth's life.

"For the last two years I've been juggling my job and business with being a volunteer leader for a Duke of Edinburgh Award group, playing hockey for my local team and running a local user group for the open source web technology we use (Joomla!). This requires me to be extremely efficient and organised, and to make the best use of technology and other resources to be able to manage my time."

Ruth is using oDesk (an online directory of professionals) to outsource aspects of the business such as database creation and advanced coding which would take her too long to do herself. By partnering with other specialists she's able to provide top-class, timely services to clients in a way that releases her time for other tasks such as business strategy.

"I'm working towards being more efficient by implementing an open-source task-management system called TaskFreak! which allows my clients to log in and view progress on the tasks relating to their job, and gives me targets to work towards. I've also upgraded my mobile phone so I can manage emails, documents and web administration on the move."

Give up the day job?

"I know I want to be self-employed as I really enjoy the freedom (and the pressures) that making your own living can bring. I am, however, also a realist. Having just moved into our first house, and looking to start a family in the next few years, now is not really the time to be making the jump into full-time self-employment. I'm confident that when the time is right, I'll be able to make the move and make a full-time living from doing what I love!"

- www.suffolkcomputerservices.co.uk

LINKS

- Joomla! www.joomla.co.uk @joomla
- ODesk www.odesk.com @odesk
- TaskFreak! www.taskfreak.com

Mobile applications developer

44

Name: Kostas Eleftheriou, Bill Rappos and Vassilis Samolis
Company name: GreatApps Ltd
Day job: Kostas is a software developer and Vassilis and Bill are students

These 3 young entrepreneurs have quite a story to tell. They operate in their spare time and across time zones, being based in the UK, Greece and the USA. They show how a 5 to 9 business can be run from anywhere in a way that certainly hasn't hindered their progress - they have served over 2 million users with paid-for and free mobile applications. This top team continues to develop best-selling apps, with their most successful to date being iSteam, which simulates the effect of condensation on a glass surface.

"iSteam gives the ability to write anything on the steamed up surface depending on how much pressure you apply with your finger, and you fog up the screen by simply breathing into your phone. Following iSteam, our next goal was to go even further into the viral app market. We developed a technology that recognises the pressure of a finger press on a touch screen like the iPhone's which we call TapForce. We implemented it in applications like Zen Piano, a piano app that sounds louder the harder you press the virtual keys, or Ice Break, an app that simulates the cracking of ice. Again, the harder you press, the bigger the cracks and the ice chunks are sent flying."

The partners think of ideas individually and then come together to share them and pick the best. iSteam was the clear winner out of 150 ideas and went on to be developed.

"We try to understand what customers want and serve them exactly that. By building smart and fun applications that have short development cycles, we can quickly move on to other ideas if they don't fare well."

They have each picked up programming skills through their respective day jobs and studies and become experts in a number of programming languages. Promotion is incorporated within app development as the team pursues their goal of having the apps advertise themselves.

"We use the internet to its full potential to create an initial buzz. We go through the works: YouTube videos of the app, press release emails to news blogs, Facebook and Twitter presence. If we've created a good application, a blog post on a site like Gizmodo will be written and that is more than enough to get people's attention."

Give up the day job?
"The plan when we formed our company was to make it a big one. We believe we have the skills to achieve this. Having already made the first steps in the corporate world, we now have contact with bigger companies and venture capitalists and we are getting ready, financially as well as academically, to give up everything else and focus on our company."

- www.greatapps.co.uk
- twitter.com/isteam
- twitter.com/greatapps

Software developer

45

Name: Tom Reader
Company name: Alver Valley Software
Day job: Computer programmer

Tom Reader came up with the idea of producing affordable and easy to use barcode software after being asked for help. His friend in need had found existing software either free and of low quality, or very expensive for something that might only be used once or twice a year.

"Although the market for barcode software is crowded, I realised I could bring some extra features at very low overheads."

Tom started Alver Valley Software in 2006 and has been building the business ever since. Tom's day job is similar to the business as he's a computer programmer but by day he works with a very different kind of software, in a different market sector and using different languages.

"My core skills are the same as in the day job but I've had to learn many skills other than computer programming to run the 5 to 9 business, like marketing, sales and customer care. It's been a great learning curve!"

Tom mainly picks up sales from his website. As well as being the point of sale for the software, the site also carries useful information for people needing to learn about producing barcodes. With this content comes

TIP

"If you're going to do something after a full day of work (and maybe after other things such as family time, housework, etc.) make sure it's something you're going to enjoy."

high ranking in the search engine results, which brings more customers. The site is also listed by a number of organisations who specify barcodes such as book publishers.

"Writing barcode software is something I enjoy working on for a while every day and it usually still leaves time for non-work hobbies. I track my time and aim to spend it on each of (a) product development, (b) marketing, and (c) admin. Realistically, I probably spend quite a bit of time on 'learning new things' too, whether it be technical such as a programming language, or how to promote my products more effectively."

Give up the day job?
"I'd love to build up my 5 to 9 business as much as possible. On the other hand, my day job is part-time and as the job and business complement each other well, I'm happy doing both for the foreseeable future."

• www.alvervalleysoftware.com

Print and web designer

Name: David Sandy
Company name: Integreat Media
Day job: Web developer for the NHS

David Sandy has been running his own business for the last few years during evenings and weekends, whilst also working in a full-time role which involves designing, developing and implementing websites and web-based applications for a large NHS trust.

"I have been totally upfront with my employer about my self-employment status and continue to put 110% effort and dedication into my employed role. Integreat Media then gets the same amount of input from me from 5 to 9! It certainly makes the day busy, but exciting!"

Since starting Integreat Media, David's business acumen has improved and he's learnt new management, business development, customer service and accounting skills; all of which help performance in his day job.

With web development being quite a flexible business model, the work can largely be done out of normal office hours. Most communication with clients is done after hours or at weekends but lunch breaks are also convenient times for catching up on calls and emails.

"A portion of annual leave can always be used when I need to visit clients or where 9 to 5 time is needed for the business. Also, some of my clients are 5 to 9'ers themselves so this is actually more convenient for them!"

David has not had to spend on advertising yet as 80% of his business is from word-of-mouth recommendations or repeat customers.

Give up the day job?
"My plans are to diversify my business skills further and I have several entrepreneurial projects lined up for the coming year which reach into new areas for me. One of the major benefits of running your own business is that you can control your direction and make your own decisions. If the business grew to a stage where it was financially stable on its own, I would consider doing it full-time to push it even further. Until then I strike an equal balance between both jobs."

- www.integreatmedia.com
- twitter.com/integreatmedia

LINKS

Promote your marketing, design, business and professional skills on platform sites where customers are visiting in search of expertise.

- Business Smiths www.businesssmiths.co.uk
- Elance www.elance.com
- Gumtree www.gumtree.com
- PeoplePerHour.com www.peopleperhour.com
- SetYourRate.com www.setyourrate.com
- Wooshii www.wooshii.com

Electrical reseller

47

Name: Arthur Guy
Company name: a star solutions
Day job: Student

Arthur Guy started 'a star solutions' when he was just 17, after working at an electronics store. He's now in his twenties, is completing a PhD at Sussex University and is developing a computer system that he hopes to roll into business number 2. He's a young entrepreneur who ably combines business and study.

"Since I was very young I've wanted to run a business, so I decided to launch a star solutions to sell a small subset of the electrical parts, leads and adapters that I'd gained experience in selling at the electronics shop. This quickly developed into the current range of audio and video leads, adapters and accessories that we now sell."

Arthur has benefited from the support of his family throughout, although as none of them had any business experience it was a steep learning curve for Arthur. He turned to the tax office on the odd occasion but as questions cropped up he would generally find the answer online.

"The business is currently run on a day-to-day basis by my mother. She handles all aspects of order fulfilment and manages the stock levels, and I deal with customer enquires as they come in as well as the accounts and

TIP

"Just do it. Starting a business isn't as hard as you think."

monitoring the necessary hardware. This only takes up a few hours each week so it isn't a problem fitting it in around university work."

Arthur is considering his options for when he leaves university. He'll either remain his own boss or get a job in a web design company so he can fill in some of the skills gaps he has as a result of learning everything on his own. If he does take that job, we're pretty sure he'll start and run a 5 to 9 business on the side!

- www.astarsolutions.co.uk
- twitter.com/ArthurGuy

LINKS

Support for graduates and students:

- Enternships: www.enternships.com
- FlyingStart: www.flyingstartonline.com
- National Council for Graduate Entrepreneurship: www.ncge.com
- National Consortium of University Entrepreneurs (NACUE): nacue.com
- School for Startups: www.schoolforstartups.co.uk
- Shell LiveWIRE: www.shell-livewire.org

Network marketer

48

Name: Karyl Iles
Company name: Arbonne International
Day job: Training facilitator

By day Karyl Iles trains and coaches individuals and by night she builds a business with networking marketing company, Arbonne, which sells Swiss-formulated, botanical skincare products.

"I actually discovered the Arbonne opportunity by accident. Over the years I've delivered training and team building to a number of network marketing companies. One of my clients referred me to Arbonne's sales director when they were looking for an experienced trainer for their first national sales conference in September 2008."

It was after delivering her session that fate played its part. Karyl was amazed to see Sue Cassidy (wife of seventies popstar David Cassidy) as the next presenter; it turns out he is a keen advocate of Arbonne products.

"I listened with great interest to Sue who is a vice president of the company. Indeed that presentation made quite an impact. I've always been encouraging others to seize opportunities and suddenly I was faced with my own – I was seriously tempted to join Arbonne, but wondered how it would affect my training business and what would my friends and family think?"

Karyl decided to try the products herself and after seeing how well they worked, she then learned about the company's Success Plan (Arbonne's version of a pay package).

"Taking everything into consideration, it was such a compelling business proposition that I decided to grab the opportunity. I worked out how I could fit Arbonne in amongst my other commitments and joined the company the following month."

Karyl spends around 12 hours a week building her Arbonne business. Sales are growing fast and Karyl is benefiting from the bonus programme that sees consultants receive rewards after reaching certain levels of sales.

"Maintaining my current growth of sales means in 3 months time Arbonne will be providing a higher income than my training business, and I'll be driving a new car which is also part of the package."

Give up the day job?

"Fortunately, I've always enjoyed my work, apart from the travelling and being away from my family. Choosing to work only with clients that are close to home will automatically result in my having less training and more Arbonne time. It's going to be a natural progression."

- www.arbonneinternational.co.uk
- twitter.com/arbonne_uk

Pet care

49

Name: Lezli and David Rees
Company name: Driving with Dogs
Day job: Both teachers

The idea for Lezli and David's business came out of basic necessity. Before owning a puppy in the UK the couple had been working abroad for some time and, as a result, knew less about UK geography than most.

"We came up with the idea after getting stuck on the motorway on a hot summer's day with a young active dog in the car. We tried bookstores for walks near motorways and when we couldn't find such a book, we decided to try the idea out as a website and see if there was any interest. The trial site started in 2006 and we had a lot of support and feedback from users to hone the content."

Driving with Dogs provides information on accessible walks whilst on the move, and because all the 400+ premium walks on the site have been created, walked and updated by the DwD team, it means that Lezli, David (and their dog, Jem) benefit from regular exercise and the opportunity to balance 9 to 5 teaching jobs with plenty of active outdoor time.

The core business is about getting drivers, with or without dogs, to take more exercise when travelling in the UK. The website and book provide 30-45 minute walks within 5 miles of all UK motorway exits. After 2 years of research and writing, the Motorway Walks book and the website have started to produce an income. The company is also generating revenue from membership fees and advertising.

The company now boasts over 1,000 members and, since publication in September 2009, more than 400 copies of *Motorway Walks* have been sold through online outlets and via bookstores. Lezli and David drive interest through their PR activities.

"We've been featured on BBC TV (Midlands Today), local BBC radio stations, and every dog-related print media we could find. We attend dog shows and events, such as Crufts and Paws in the Park, and promote the website with high-quality printed postcards."

Lezli and David have also hired in help from a PR agency specialising in dog products. This has boosted awareness of the business and led to feature articles in camping, caravanning and motor publications that they couldn't have reached themselves.

"We have also brought a web developer onto the team. This has enabled us to focus on our core business which is content development."

The couple are using Web 2.0 technology to facilitate greater interactivity on the site with members now able to contribute walks, dog-friendly pubs and beaches to the site, and rate and comment on existing content. Technology also applies to their printed material.

"*Motorway Walks* is published on demand which means we can update the content electronically at any point and there is no wastage of resources as the books are only printed for definite sales."

- www.drivingwithdogs.co.uk

Give up the day job?

Lezli: "Yes, probably over a 5-year period. I like the day job and plan to phase it out gently as website sales increase. Although if sales really took off I would definitely give up the day-job quicker."

David: "No. His initial technical input has achieved a personal goal and he's more day-job focused now."

For information and links on self-publishing books, see page 36.

50 Rare breed pig farmer

Name: Gwen Howell
Company name: Pigs in Clover
Day job: Estate agent

"We never intended to become pig farmers," says Gwen Howell, "we're estate agents, running a busy agency, and we just wanted a couple of pigs for ourselves, one for bacon and one for pork."

Little did Gwen and husband Steve know that a plan to buy two pigs would lead to a thriving part-time business. The Howells happened across an ad in their local paper for some Saddleback pigs. When Steve went to see them, they were being kept in bad conditions in a concrete bunker so he bought the lot. All ten pigs. The Howells got to work building an ark (home for pigs) with a decent-sized run and on 10 March 2009, their first pigs arrived.

"On 12 March, Steve went on a pig-keeping course, run by Tony York, which was an absolute stroke of luck, as it turned out that Tony is a doyen of the pig world, hugely respected, and enormously helpful to new pig keepers. He fired Steve up so much on that course that Steve metamorphosed overnight into an avid rare breed pig breeder. One month later I did the same course and was equally enthused."

Since then Gwen and Steve have invested heavily in arks and fencing and now have over 70 pigs. The company supplies pork to private individuals and several local restaurants. There has even been some common ground with their day job.

"I dress in a suit and high heels in the day, then I go home and change into old jeans and wellies, to become my alter ego – pig farmer. I deal mostly with the pig marketing so the skill set is the same and I use all the same equipment as I do at the agency – computers, printers, laminator, etc, etc."

Pigs in Clover has quickly developed a high profile. The most recent coverage being on the back of their trampolining pig, Scarlett, who was entered for *Britain's Got Talent*. This led to appearances on the *Alan Titchmarsh Show*, Sky, and the BBC. The company has sold sausages and pork to customers through Facebook and is now supplying a Michelin-starred restaurant. This business knows no bounds when it comes to getting word out and about.

Give up the day job?
"I would love to. I've been doing it since 1983 (with a short break to be a rave promoter and underground magazine publisher in the early 90s, and to do a degree). I like being at home, but think I would miss the office, especially in the winter. I'd probably get fat if I stayed home, as I like to cook big, satisfying meals when I get a day off, using all our own produce. Mind you, digging the veg patch burns off the calories."

* www.pigsinclover.co.uk
* twitter.com/pigsincloveruk

TIP

"Grow a business that you really love and enjoy so the hours you spend on it are not a chore. And don't forget to make time for your family, and yourself."

Home business opportunities

If you'd rather buy in to a proven idea and be your own boss whilst also being part of a team, becoming a franchise or consultant could be the route to take.

In no particular order, here are my top 15 franchise options for 5 to 9'ers.

1. My Secret Kitchen (case study: page 114)

My Secret Kitchen was the brainchild of husband-and-wife team, Phil and Clare Moran. This dynamic duo are fast signing up consultants who host food-tasting parties and earn commission on sales of products made at the party.

Sound tempting?

- www.mysecretkitchen.co.uk

2. Jamie at Home (case study: page 112)

A party plan opportunity from Jamie Oliver that involves "going to parties to help non-cooks choose great kit while introducing those who already know their stuff to a range of beautiful things for their home".

Jamie at Home consultants earn commission on everything that's sold at their home parties and receive full support and training from the central HQ team. Consultants have joined from a range of professions including policewomen, nurses, scientists, lawyers and mums.

- www.jamieathome.com

3. Pampered Chef

The Pampered Chef is a direct-seller of kitchen tools with 2,900 consultants in the UK. Consultants host parties to sell the tools at in home cooking shows and earn a commission on sales. The guests learn time-saving cooking techniques and sample easy-to-prepare recipes. Everyone wins!

- www.pamperedchef.co.uk

4. House Tutor

House Tutor is the franchised home interior design business set up by Sally McIlroy. By training to become a tutor, you're set up over 10 weeks with the tools to run your own home-interior-design business with the central office of the company on hand to provide support. All House Tutors hold a design qualification and are carefully selected.

- www.housetutor.co.uk

5. Girlie Gardening

Turn a passion for the great outdoors into extra income to spend indoors by becoming a party planner for Girlie Gardening. The company was started by Helen James and Cathy Caudwell Todd who wanted to bring glamour to women gardeners across the UK. Consultants host parties and distribute catalogues to sell products including gloves and garden gift sets.

- www.girliegardening.com

6. Avon

Avon is the biggest direct-selling beauty company in the world with over 5 million representatives. In the UK Avon has an army of sales reps that's bigger than our armed forces. That's because Avon offers an opportunity to work hours that suit and an income that pleases; a perfect 5 to 9 opportunity.

- www.avon.com

7. VIE at home

Formerly known as Virgin Vie at Home, this company offers a work-at-home, in-your-own-hours opportunity that involves selling cosmetics to friends and family. No experience is required but once started and as sales build, many consultants choose to make their VIE-at-home business a full-time career.

- www.vieathome.com

8. Flori Roberts

Flori Roberts is a cosmetics brand developed exclusively for women of colour. Having been established in the US since 1965, the company is now coming to the UK and looking for consultants who want to work part-time hours. The opportunity is to build a direct-selling network of friends and colleagues through home-based 'Beauty Hour' parties. As a consultant you earn between 25% and 40% on every sale and the host receives free products.

- www.floriroberts.co.uk

9. Arbonne (case study: page 149)

The Arbonne strapline says it all: "You're in business for yourself, but not by yourself." Case-study Karyl Isles tells the story of how she started out and how income from her Arbonne business is overtaking earnings from her day job. The products are Swiss-formulated and high quality, and support from the central marketing and business development team is top class.

- www.arbonneinternational.co.uk

10. My Little Wrapper

Have your part-time business all wrapped up; you buy a business kit (current cost £999 for the mini pack) and then produce personalised wrappers for chocolate bars. The bars can then be sold to someone hosting an event, as a corporate gift, as wedding favours or for any commemorative occasion – the only limit is your imagination.

- www.getmylittlewrapper.co.uk

11. Tish Tash Toys

This one is for parents interested in earning extra income by selling toys at parties, coffee mornings, playgroups, nurseries, fairs and fêtes. The company has over 100 network marketing sales staff who earn commission on everything they sell and benefit from discounts on toys they buy themselves.

- www.tishtashtoys.com

12. Music bugs

If music is your passion, how about a franchise running fun, friendly and interactive music and singing classes? Music Bugs franchisees have high demand for their sessions so you'd be starting a business with a proven market and track record.

- www.musicbugs.co.uk

13. Funky Feet

Funky Feet delivers dance parties and workshops to children and young people throughout the UK and the way the company is expanding is through franchising. Applicants for this opportunity should have at least 2 years experience of working with children and a clear ability in dance. Franchisees receive a dedicated territory plus training and ongoing support.

- www.funkyfeetunlimited.co.uk

14. Usborne Books

Be your own boss, and build a business around your family with Usborne Books at Home. The company sells children's books and, as a franchisee, you can sell Usborne books wherever and whenever suits you, and even take the children along too! Sellers earn up to 26% on sales from day 1, there's no prior selling experience required and all Usborne organisers have a network of other Organisers to approach for help and advice.

- www.usborne.com

15. Kleeneze

Kleeneze is a leading home-shopping company offering a wide range of household, health and beauty items, sold through a national network of shopping specialists who are busy building their own successful home businesses, many in their spare time.

The company offers an opportunity to anyone over the age of 18 who wants to earn extra income by making sales, and recruiting friends and family to do the same.

- www.kleeneze.net

III. Next steps

You have your idea.
Now what?

It's time to analyse
the idea, tell the boss,
get set-up, make some
noise about your
venture, make a sale,
and keep those sales
coming in.

From idea to business

You have your idea. To turn it into a business requires some research, followed by a straightforward exercise in turning that research into a plan. Here's how to go about it.

Research

Research your potential customers, the competition and a price point by visiting competitor's sites and trying their products, online trade sites/forums, reading reports, and seeking intelligence from experts. Look for data and comments that will answer the following questions:

How big is the market?
- What is the number of potential customers you can serve, and how do these customers like to be served?
- What are their characteristics, spending patterns and who are their key influencers?

Who is currently serving my market?
- Where are your potential customers going for their goods and services?
- What do they like about what they're getting and, more importantly, what do they dislike as this opens up opportunities for you to improve on the status quo?

In view of the above, what price can I charge for my product/service?

Price yourself at a rate that's competitive with other providers in the market, that takes into account the amount of time, personal service and added value you offer, and that will turn a profit at the end of the day!

SWOT Analysis

With your idea, and now your research in-hand that supports your idea, prepare a SWOT analysis. This stands for: Strengths, Weaknesses, Opportunities, Threats and can be completed as follows:

Strengths
What are my strengths?
- What can I do better than anyone else?
- What resources do I have?
- What's my unique selling point (USP)?

Weaknesses
What are my weaknesses?
- What should I avoid?
- Where do I lack skills?
- What might hinder my success?

Opportunities
What opportunities do I see?
- Does my idea tap into any trends?
- Are there any emerging technologies that could help my idea?
- Has there been anything in the news related to my idea?

Threats
What are the threats?
- What's my competition?
- Does changing technology affect my idea?

IMOFF

You're almost ready to embark on your entrepreneurial journey; write up the findings from your research in the form of a brief business plan that will act as your route map along the way. It's easy to remember what to include in a plan if you think of it in terms of 'I'm Off' or IMOFF:

- **Idea**
  What's your idea?

- **Market**
  Who will be your customers or clients? And who is your competition?

- **Operations**
  How will you develop the idea, promote it, and provide good customer service?

- **Financials**
  Can you earn more than you spend so the business makes a profit?

- **Friends**
  Do you have a support network on hand for when you need business advice? Are there complementary businesses you've identified with whom partnerships are a possibility?

Have these as headings in your plan and sure enough you've taken a big step closer to becoming your own boss.

Executive Summary

Summarise what's in the rest of the plan. Something like this:

The vision for ABC is to become the leading company for selling xxx to xxx. This plan sets out how the vision will be achieved in the period from 2010-2012. It outlines the product on offer, provides data on the customer market and shows how an experienced founder will have the company operating profitably within the first 3 months.

Having identified a clear gap in the market, I'm excited about the opportunity to start and build a successful business that will offer a quality product and service to a well-defined market.

A. Smith
Founder, Company ABC

The Idea

Include here your 'elevator pitch'; what is your product and how will it benefit the customer.

Company ABC
Business Plan
2010 — 2012

(This business plan is for a 2-year cycle. You may choose to do a 12-month plan, or up to 5 years!)

Contents

The Market

Customers

Who will be your customers? Include the number of them, their demographic profile, geographic location, social and education background; essentially any strong data that shows you know your audience.

Competition

Who is selling a similar product/service? How do you differ from them and what is your unique selling point?

You can do this by producing a table that lists the competition and you. Outline what makes you stand out in the market; is it that your service will be online, that you'll charge a different price, have an innovative marketing approach or offer the service with a special extra twist?

Operations

The CEO

You have come up with the idea for the business and you've done your research on the market. Now it's time for the reader to know a bit about you! Note your background, skills, experience and any credentials for running this business.

Sourcing

If this applies to your business, refer to how you'll source your product/service. You may be making it yourself!

Business plan

Every business needs to write a full business plan to lay out their goals, ambitions, and means of achieving them.

Sales & Marketing

How will you promote what you offer to your customers? Include a brief sales and marketing plan with headings like this:

- Press — how many press releases do you plan to distribute each year and to which press channels; newspapers, magazines, radio, etc?
- Online — will you have your own blog/website? Mention other sites that you'll approach for reciprocal links
- Partners — what about marketing tie-ups with other companies selling to the same audience?

You know where your customers are so let your marketing plan show that you'll reach them in print, online and even in the streets!

Systems

You've sourced the service/product and told customers about it. Refer here to the process customers will go through to buy from you and the systems you'll have in place to deliver in time and on budget. Systems that may include online ordering & payment, a professional call-handling service to take orders or maybe some specific software.

Friends & Family

In starting and growing your business, will you call on friends & family for advice? If so, refer to this here; mention your board of advisors, your experts-on-call, your support network!

TIP

Further information

For more information on business planning, read my other book *Spare Room Start Up: How to start a business from home* or visit enterprisenation.com.

Financials

Last but not least come the figures. Make this as basic as possible and it's probably best to do it in table form:

	Year 1	Year 2
Revenue	xxxx	xxxx
Overheads		
• Office rent	0	0
• Salary	(xx)	(xx)
• Stock	(xx)	(xx)
• Technology	(xx)	(xx)
• Marketing	(xx)	(xx)
• Travel & expenses	(xx)	(xx)
Projected profit	xxxx	xxxx

Drawing up a simple financial forecast will highlight any need to borrow money or look for funding.

Setting up your business

Don't give up the day job

When planning your 5 to 9 business one of the first things you need to consider is your day job.

Do I have to tell the boss?

At some stage in the planning process, this question will come to mind. My advice? Follow the path taken by most of the 5 to 9'ers profiled here by checking your employment contract and having a conversation with your employer. Here's how to go about it.

The contract

If you have written terms and conditions of employment they are likely to contain reference to the pursuit of personal business ventures outside your contracted working hours. The clauses to look out for include 'the employee's duties and obligations' and what is commonly known as 'whole time and effort'. These clauses require the employee to devote the whole of their time, attention and abilities to the business of the employer.

If your contract contains these or similar clauses, don't despair, as it doesn't necessarily mean you can't pursue your business. Many employment contracts are drafted using standard templates with little consideration to personal circumstance. You know your job better than anyone, so if you don't think your business venture will affect the way you do your job, it probably won't and your employer will recognise this.

Having checked how things stand in the contract, it's time to talk things through with your boss.

The conversation

Treat it as an amicable and informal conversation to gauge your employer's initial reaction.

I asked Patrick Lockton, a qualified lawyer and head of Matrix Law Group, for his take on the matter and advice on how employees should go about having this conversation:

"When you approach your employer, be prepared to negotiate, be flexible and compromise. If you think it appropriate, make it clear your business venture will in no shape or form affect your ability to do your job or affect your employer's interests. If anything, it will make you a better, more confident and experienced employee and it will not cost your employer a thing."

Patrick goes on to say:

"After having such a conversation, you can do one of two things:

1. if your employer has not expressed any concerns about your intentions and you have no concerns of your own, disclose your intentions to your employer anyway. Treat it as something you want to do for the sake of clarity and for the record, as opposed to something you want their permission for; or

2. if your employer has expressed concerns, try and negotiate a package that you are both happy with. Address their concerns, agree some ground rules and get their permission in writing. Give your employer as much helpful information as possible. If you are going to need some time off or to change your hours then this is the time to bring it up.

"Always take written notes so you don't forget what was said and so you can remind your employer what was agreed."

So long as you're not competing with your employer or breaching their trust, you shouldn't have any problem at all in pursuing your 5 to 9 ambitions. After all, as Patrick says, your employer benefits from all the new skills you're picking up, and it doesn't cost them a penny in training or resources!

With thanks to Patrick Lockton, Matrix Law Group, www.matrixlawgroup.com.

With your employment affairs now in order, it's time to do the same with your business affairs.

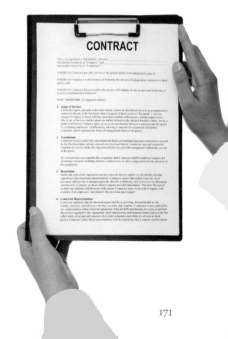

Working 5 to 9 and the taxman

The rules on tax and working 5 to 9 are pretty clear-cut. You are required to register with HM Revenue & Customs (HMRC) as soon as you start earning from any business activity. You can choose to register as self-employed, as a partnership, or as a limited company. Each has their own filing requirements as shown below. Talk to an accountant about the structure that is best for your business.

Self-employed

This status means you are working for yourself; you keep all the profits and are solely liable for any debts. The calculation of tax and National Insurance owing is done through self-assessment.

You either need to complete a form CWF1, or simply call the newly self-employed business helpline. It should be done within three months of undertaking your first piece of self-employed work in order to avoid a fine.

- Form CWF1 www.hmrc.gov.uk/forms/cwf1.pdf
- Helpline for the newly self-employed 0845 915 4515

It's not onerous to complete the form and, once registered, you'll be classified as self-employed and sent a self-assessment tax return each year, which you complete showing your income and expenses from self-employment as well as details of your employment.

You will be subject to tax and national insurance on any profits you make, but the good news is that any losses incurred can be offset against your employed income, which could even result in a tax rebate.

TIP

Self-Assessment Tax Return deadlines
- Paper tax return should be received by HMRC by 31 October.
- Online tax return should be completed by 31 January (giving you an extra 3 months).

If turnover (i.e. sales) remains below £30,000 (in the 2009/10 tax year), you are not required to submit detailed accounts to HM Revenue & Customs. Instead, you simply complete 3 boxes on your tax return:

- Sales
- Expenditure
- Net Profit

If an accountant is doing this for you, the simplicity of the job brings down the cost of the work so, for both business and personal tax returns, accountancy fees should be no more than £100-£150 a year.

- Leaflet SE1 – Are you thinking of working for yourself? www.hmrc.gov.uk/leaflets/se1.pdf
- HMRC Helping you understand Self Assessment and your Tax Return http://www.hmrc.gov.uk/sa

Tax responsibilities for the self-employed

Your turnover determines the forms that need to be filed with HMRC. Current rules for the 10/11 tax year are:

1. Below £30,000
   At this level a taxpayer is usually only required to submit a 'Short' Tax Return (SA200). HMRC will normally issue a Short Return, based on your figures for the previous tax year. That said, when completing a return online, you will be asked if your turnover is below £30,000. More info can be found at www.hmrc.gov.uk/sa/shorttaxreturn.htm.
2. £30,000 to £67,000
   At this level, you are required to complete a full Self-Assessment Tax Return (SA100). Part of this is the Self-Employment section. If turnover is below £67,000 you can choose whether to show expenses as a single figure or broken down by category.
3. Over £67,000
   Above this level, you are required to complete both a full SA100 and a detailed Self-Employment section.

Partnership

According to HMRC, a partnership is where:

"Two or more people set up a business. Each partner is personally responsible for all the business debts, even if the debt was caused by another partner. As partners, each pays income tax on their share of the business profits through Self-Assessment, as well as National Insurance."

In terms of filing requirements, each partner should complete a partnership supplementary page as part of their individual Self Assessment Tax Return. This is in addition to a Partnership Return that has to be submitted by one nominated partner and show each partner's share of profits/losses.

Limited company

Limited companies exist in their own right, with the company's finances distinct from the personal finances of the owners. What this means is that the company is liable for any debts, not the individual owners, as is the case if you are self-employed or in a partnership.

In April 2008 it became legal to form and run a limited company with just one person, without the need to involve anyone else (prior to this by law you also needed a company secretary). You can form a new limited company by registering with Companies House (www.companieshouse.gov.uk) or by using a company creation agent which can be done online from as little as £25 with UK Plc (www.uk-plc.net) or The Company Warehouse (www.thecompanywarehouse.co.uk).

TIP

Partnership Tax Return deadlines
- Paper tax return should be received by HMRC by 31st October.
- Online tax return should be completed by 31st January (giving you an extra three months).

As well as registering with Companies House, you also need to let HMRC know you are operating as a limited company. You can do this by completing a CT41G form.

- CT41G form
  http://bit.ly/de4qi9

You will also need to set up and register a PAYE scheme as you are an employee of the company.

- Register PAYE scheme
  www.hmrc.gov.uk/newemployers
- New Employer's Helpline 0845 60 70 143

In terms of filing requirements, you should complete a Self-Assessment Company Tax Return at the end of the accounting period. The return will show the company's taxable profits and whether any corporation tax is owed and can be filed online at www.hmrc.gov.uk/ct

The return should also be filed with Companies House to comply with The Companies Act 2006. This can be done free of charge using Companies House online WebFiling service https://ewf.companieshouse.gov.uk

Expenses

On your returns, you can claim wear-and-tear allowances (capital allowances) on any equipment you buy, and, also an element of your expenses for working from home – although, in the case of 5 to 9'ers, as you are mainly 'based' at home, rather than actually working extensively from home, these will be restricted. But it all helps. You can also claim travelling expenses, subsistence and a proportion of your phone calls.

> **TIP**
>
> **Company Tax Return deadlines**
> Whereas filing deadlines for Self-Assessment and Partnership Tax Returns are specific dates, that is not the case with Company Tax Returns which must be filed 12 months after the end of your company's Corporation Tax accounting period.

VAT

Whichever tax status you choose, if your business turns over more than £68,000 (in the 2009/10 tax year) or you think your turnover will soon exceed this amount, you should also register for Value Added Tax (VAT). You can voluntarily register at any time; being VAT-registered can bring credibility with certain customers but adding VAT to your invoices may make you more expensive than competitors and you will have to file a VAT return 4 times a year.

- HMRC *How and when to register for VAT* www.hmrc.gov.uk/vat/start/register

Even if your accounts are very simple, do seek professional advice if possible, particularly as the rules and regulations can change frequently and without warning.

- HM Revenue & Customs, *Starting in Business* www.hmrc.gov.uk/startingup
- Tax Help – to register a new business www.businesslink.gov.uk/taxhelp
- Enterprise Nation's top accountant, Alan Young 1staddition.blogspot.com

Business Rates

The final form of tax to bear in mind is business rates. If you have applied for planning permission or your Local Authority is aware you are running a business from home, they may try to charge you business rates on the part of the house being used for business purposes, as opposed to council tax. Business rates are different in each area and something that should be agreed with your Local Authority.

- My Business Rates www.mybusinessrates.gov.uk

Do I need planning permission?

You'll only need planning permission to base the business at home if you answer 'yes' to any of these questions:

- will my home no longer be used mainly as a private residence?
- will my business result in a marked rise in traffic or people calling?
- will my business involve any activities unusual in a residential area?
- will my business disturb the neighbours at unreasonable hours or create other forms of nuisance such as noise or smells?

If your house is pretty much going to remain a house, with your business quietly accommodated within it, then permission won't be required. If you're unsure, contact your local council to seek their views.

- www.planningportal.gov.uk

Make some noise

STOP PRESS

5 to 9'ers make the headlines

Gwen Howell from Pigs in Clover has had her name in most of the major papers after entering one of her pigs for *Britain's Got Talent*. The pig's talent? Trampolining!

STOP PRESS

5 to 9'ers make the headlines

Janan Leo from CocoRose London has been in *The Sunday Times*, on *Working Lunch* and *Reuters TV* after journalists heard the story of how she works on rail company products by day and sells shoes across the globe from a shoedoir at the top of her home by night.

Decide on a name for your new business and ensure it's the name on everyone's lips. Here's how to go about it.

Issue a press release

The first step is to write a press release and send it to journalists covering your line of business at newspapers and magazines (both local and national). Get their names and contact details from the publication, online or from a media database, and send each one a personal email.

Your press release should have an attention-grabbing headline, the main facts in the first sentence and evidence and quotes from as high-profile people and companies as possible in the main body of the text. Also include great quality images wherever you can to lift the piece and put a face to the brand.

You could also use a press-release distribution service to secure wider exposure. My personal favourite is Response Source (www.responsesource.com) but there's also PR Newswire (www.prnewswire.co.uk) and PRWeb (www.prweb.com).

Enter awards

Many award schemes are free to enter and are targeted at young start-up businesses. Writing the entry will help to clarify your goals and vision, and winning will bring profile and prizes.

To find out about upcoming awards, visit www.awardsintelligence.co.uk.

Register on Enterprise Nation to receive news and enter our own annual Home Business Awards!

Host an event

Invite the press to come and meet you. This doesn't have to be an expensive affair; the secret is partnering with others who would benefit from being in front of your audience. Approach a venue and ask if you can host at no cost, in exchange for the venue receiving profile. Do the same with caterers. Then give invited guests a reason to attend – have a theme, an interesting speaker, a launch announcement, something that will grab their attention and encourage them to attend. Make use of free online services such as Eventbrite (www.eventbrite.com) to send out invites and receive rsvp's.

Tell your story

Look for every opportunity to tell your story. When attending events, ask questions and announce your name and company clearly. If there are topical news items, then respond to them, e.g. if there's a postal strike, has this affected your business as it relies on delivering products? If so, call up the local radio and press and tell them. Follow business shows and media channels on Twitter so you can respond to opportunities as they are posted.

Media channels to follow:
- @the_4th_floor (BBC Radio 1)
- @e_nation
- @findatvexpert
- @jiminthemorning (who must be the most prolific twittering radio DJ around!)
- @workinglunch

STOP PRESS

5 to 9'ers make the headlines
Uncle Wilco of Readersheds appeared on Chris Evans' BBC radio show after securing Chris as a judge in his Shed of the Year competition, along with fellow judges inventor Trevor Baylis and property expert Sarah Beeny.

TIP

The power of the image
Have a professional photo taken of you/ your products/your work environment.

With a powerful image, you're much more likely to be covered and have readers notice you. If you don't know a professional photographer (or don't have the budget to spare), approach the local art college and ask if the students would like to take your picture to display in their portfolio. Then smile. Everyone wins!

Link request
If you're being featured online ask the writer if they can include a live link to your site. That way, readers can be on your site within a click.

Look in the lifestyle magazines and turn to the page where they ask readers to submit their story. Submit yours!

Be available

This is possibly the toughest one for the 5 to 9'er. A journalist calls during the day (whilst you're at work) and wants a response. What do you do? Agree a time to talk that suits you or quietly slip into the corridor or outside? Whatever you do, whenever possible do agree to speak. Profile brings attention and credibility which in turn brings customers and it gets you on the media's list of contacts.

Tell us your story

So we can profile you on Enterprise Nation and consider you for media requests.

Print

Print is far from dead so get yourself some business cards, postcards, promotional flyers to hand out at business events, social occasions, and to just about anyone you meet! Have fun with designing your cards at sites like www.moo.com where 200 cards can be bought for less than £40. For another online service there's Vistaprint (www.vistaprint.co.uk) or if you'd prefer to order cards face-to-face, try the print and copy centres in Staples stores (www.staples.co.uk), Printing.com outlets (www.printing.com), or Mail Boxes Etc. units (www.mbe.co.uk).

Online

This is where the fun starts. Many of the profiled 5 to 9'ers have marketed themselves exclusively online and it's reaping rewards. Create accounts and profiles, spend 30 minutes or so each day keeping them maintained and enjoy meeting new contacts and watching orders come in. Here's how to become known online without spending a single penny.

Twitter

Visit www.twitter.com, create an account, start to follow friends and contacts (and their followers) and get tweeting. Follow Mark Shaw's steps for Twitter success on page 182.

- Cost: free

Facebook

Visit www.facebook.com, create an account, invite friends and contacts to join your group and get promoting. Also take on board San Sharma's secrets to Facebook success on page 186.

- Cost: free

LinkedIn

Visit www.linkedin.com, create an account and start connecting with existing contacts and finding new ones. See our top tips from LinkedIn on page 184.

- Cost: free (option to upgrade to a business account which is a paid-for package)

Flickr

Join www.flickr.com and promote yourself in a visual way by uploading photos of you and your products or service, and maybe even a few shots of happy customers.

- Cost: free (option to upgrade to a pro account which is a paid-for package)

YouTube

Start your own channel on www.youtube.com then upload and share video clips of your business or expertise. Footage can even be filmed for free if you have a webcam in your laptop. Alternatively, consider investing in a Flip camera [see page 206].

- Cost: free

Budget required for online promotion: £0
And all these steps can be taken between the hours of 5 and 9.

TIP

Run a poll with, for example, surveymonkey.com, which is free to use, and publish the results via a press release and online. The media loves good polls!

How to be a success on Twitter

Twitter expert Mark Shaw shares his 4 top tips that will have you tweeting like a pro.

1. Be committed
Add a good photo, perhaps a bespoke background, your website URL and an interesting bio. Try and differentiate yourself and make sure the bio contains keywords so others can find you.

2. Be consistent
Show up each day, and tweet, even if time is short. It's more important to do a small amount each day than lots one day and then nothing for a week or so.

3. Be interesting
Try and tweet 3 types of messages: social chit-chat; the sharing of resources, links, tools, info, ideas and opinions; and tweets that answer questions which demonstrate your knowledge. Aim for a good balance.

4. Be interested
Engage with others by answering questions and joining in. Find conversations to enter into via search.twitter.com and Retweet (RT) other people's messages if they are of interest to you and your followers. It's not about selling things but it is all about building your brand and credibility.

Mark Shaw

- twitter.com/markshaw
- www.markshaw.biz

Top tips from LinkedIn

Present a full picture of yourself

Make sure you add a professional picture so people can easily recognise you and take some time to complete your profile. You'll show up in more search results the more information you provide about your experience and skills. While doing this, picture yourself at a conference or client meeting. How do you introduce yourself? That's your authentic voice and that's what should come across in writing.

Build connections

Connections are one of the most important aspects of your brand – the company you keep reflects the quality of your brand. Identify connections that will add to your credibility and pursue them.

Write a personal tagline

The line of text under your name is the first thing people see in your profile. It follows your name in search hit lists. It's your brand. Ensure it's something that at a glance describes who you are.

Put your elevator pitch to work

Go back to your conference introduction. That 30-second description, the essence of who you are and what you do, is a personal elevator pitch. Use it in the Summary section to engage readers. You've got 5-10 seconds to capture their attention.

Point out your skills

Think of the Specialties field as your personal search engine optimiser, a way to refine the ways people find and remember you. Mention particular abilities and interests, even a note of humour or passion.

Explain your experience

Briefly say what the company does. After you've introduced yourself, describe what you do and what your company does. Use those clear, succinct phrases here.

Distinguish yourself from the crowd

Use the Additional Information section to round out your profile with a few key interests. Maybe you belong to a trade association or an interest group; if you're an award-winner, add prestige by listing that here.

Ask and answer questions

Thoughtful questions and useful answers build your credibility. Make a point of answering questions in your field to establish your expertise and raise your visibility. You may need answers to a question of your own later on.

Recommendations

Pat your own back and others' too. Get recommendations from colleagues and clients who will speak credibly about your performance and make meaningful comments when recommending others.

Source: LinkedIn
www.linkedin.com

Manage your personal life, day job and 5 to 9 business on Facebook

In 1999, there were 350 million people on the internet. Today, that many people are on Facebook alone, so a good number of your customers could be there too.

So how do you separate your personal and professional lives on Facebook? And what do you do when you have two professions – a day job and a business?

By working 5 to 9 you'll know about managing multiple identities, but with Facebook you have the tools to do so – and it doesn't involve signing up for multiple accounts. To manage your personal life, day job and 5 to 9 business, all you need to do is follow these 3 simple steps:.

1. Sign up

To sign up for Facebook all you need to provide is your name, email address, gender and birthday and you can even hide some of these details from your profile, if you wish. Go to www.facebook.com to get started.

2. Manage your privacy settings

Although running a 5 to 9 business needn't be a cloak-and-dagger affair, there may be some things you don't want your friends or colleagues to see – or things that just might not interest them.

Change how people find and see your profile by choosing Privacy Settings from the Settings drop-down menu. You can control who can see your profile and post to your wall, who can contact you on Facebook and see your contact details, and how your profile can be found by search engines like Google.

You can also control who sees the things you post to Facebook, from photos and videos, to events and links. Look for the padlock icon to adjust settings on a per-post basis.

3. Set up a page to promote your business

Facebook Pages may look like regular Profiles, but they're much more powerful as a way to engage with customers and their friends.

A Facebook Page is like a profile for your business, except with fans rather than friends. When fans interact with your Page their actions are published to the News Feed, which is an excellent way to promote your business to friends of friends and their friends too! Think of it as word-of-mouth marketing, only completely free and happening online.

To create a Facebook Page look for Ads and Pages in your Applications menu.

San Sharma

- www.sansharma.com
- twitter.com/sansharma

Getting out and about

You're starting to get known in the media and online and now it's time to get and about and introduce yourself to customers and contacts face-to-face.

Join a group or club

Signing up to a local business club or network is good for business and your social life. You get together to do deals but also end up making friends. And one of the biggest plus points for 5 to 9'ers is that many events are held during hours when you can attend. Check out these national business networks to find your natural fit.

- **1230 TWC** Events for women in business www.1230.co.uk

- **4Networking** National network of business breakfast groups www.4networking.biz

- **The Athena Network** Networking organisation for women in business www.theathenanetwork.com

- **Business Scene** Hosts regional and national networking events as well as hosting an online directory of over 10,000 events across the UK www.business-scene.com

- **Ecademy** National site with local and regional meet-ups – www.ecademy.com

- **Jelly** An American import which encourages casual gatherings of coworkers, with events held in people's homes, the local coffee shop or other informal spaces. The idea is you meet in relaxed surroundings and creative ideas are stimulated from the experience – www.workatjelly.com

Creating the right first impression

You're about to attend your first networking event. Create a sparkling impression from the start.

- Enter the room with your head held high
- Approach someone who is standing alone or edge close to a small group
- Offer a firm handshake and clearly state your name and business name
- Remember the other person's name by making a connection (the person is called Peter so you think of Peter Pan) or ask them to repeat or spell their name if appropriate
- Ask about their business (showing interest in the reply) and maintaining eye contact (as opposed to peering over their shoulder to see who else is at the party!)
- Make a common connection (Peter is a personal fitness trainer so you mention your current running regime)
- Offer your elevator pitch, i.e. describe your business in one sentence
- Exchange business cards
- When the time is right, move on politely
- Follow up after the event with an email to confirm the opportunities identified

- **School for Startups**
  Headed by serial entrepreneur Doug Richard, School for Startups travels the UK hosting events for anyone considering starting a business. Gems from Doug's presentations are broadcast via S4STV.
  www.schoolforstartups.co.uk

- **Women in Rural Enterprise (WIRE)**
  Networking and business club for rural women in business – www.wireuk.org

- **First Friday** A free business networking event held monthly - an informal gathering in a welcoming environment
  www.firstfriday-network.co.uk

There are also chambers, associations, trade groups and enterprise agencies who host regular events:

- **British Chambers of Commerce**
  www.britishchambers.org.uk
- **Business Link** www.businesslink.gov.uk
- **Enterprise UK** www.enterpriseuk.org
- **Federation of Small Businesses**
  www.fsb.org.uk
- **Forum of Private Business** www.fpb.org
- **NFEA**, the national enterprise network
  www.nfea.com
- **Professional Contractors Group (PCG)**
  www.pcg.org.uk
- **She's Ingenious** www.shesingenious.org

National bodies that hold events and offer support at certain stages in your entrepreneurial career include:

- **National Council for Graduate Entrepreneurship** A body responsible for encouraging new start-ups and an entrepreneurial mindset amongst students and graduates up to 5 years out of education. Hosts a programme of regular events and rallies called FlyingStart that attract thousands of attendees. www.ncge.com www.flyingstartonline.com

- **National Enterprise Academy** Started by *Dragons' Den* entrepreneur Peter Jones, the Academy offers a full-time educational course and qualification in enterprise and entrepreneurship for 16-19 year olds. www.thenea.org

- **PRIME** (The Prince's Initiative for Mature Enterprise) A network for the over 50s that provides free information, events and training. PRIME also offers loans through an innovative scheme with online lender Zopa and the charitable arm of Bank of America.
  www.primeinitiative.co.uk
  www.primebusinessclub.co.uk

Approach local contacts

Whether it be contacting the local school, businesses or shops, get in touch and offer to speak or provide demonstrations. The only cost is your time yet the payback is plenty of goodwill and possibly new custom.

TIP

Guidelines for displaying at farmers' markets

Retailers selling food must register with their local environmental health officer (EHO) who can be contacted via your local council (see www.direct.gov.uk). There is a requirement to have product and public liability insurance. The recommended minimum is £5 million and an annual policy is available for under £100.

Sources of information:
- www.farmersmarkets.net
- www.farma.org.uk

Attend trade shows

Promote your brand by attending the shows your customers attend. Research the best shows by reading industry magazines and visiting online forums where people in your sector are talking.

Tradeshow tactics

Before the event

- **Negotiate a good deal** – If you're prepared to wait it out, the best deals on stands can be had days before the event is starting. The closer the date the better the price you'll negotiate as the sales team hurry to get a full house.

- **Tell people you're going** – Circulate news that you'll be at the event through online networks (giving your location or stand number) and issue a press release if you're doing something newsworthy at the event, maybe launching a new product, having a guest appearance, running a competition, etc.

At the event

- **Be clear on the offer** – Determine what you are selling at the show and let this be consistent across show materials; from pop-up stands to flyers. Be creative with the stand to keep costs low. Pop-up banners can be bought for £45 each from companies like Demonprint (www.demonprint.co.uk) and a supply of mouth-watering brownies to entice visitors can be acquired from Gower Cottage Brownies (www.gowercottagebrownies.co.uk).

- **Collect data** –Find ways to collect attendee's names and details. Offer a prize in exchange for business cards or take details in exchange for a follow-up information pack or offer. Some events also offer the facility to scan the details from the delegates badges (for a fee).

- **Take friends/family** – Invite a supportive team. If you're busy talking to a potential customer, you'll want others on the stand who can be doing the same. If there's time, get to know the exhibitors around you.

- **Be prepared** – Wear comfortable shoes, bring some spare clothes and pack your lunch – if you're busy there may not be time to spend buying food and drink!

After the event
- **Follow-up** – Within a couple of days of returning from the show contact the people who expressed interest so that interest can be turned into sales.

- **Plan ahead** – If the show delivered a good return, contact the organisers and ask to be considered for a speaking slot or higher profile at the next event, and confirm your willingness to be a case study testimonial story in any post-show promotion.

Tech toolkit for the 5 to 9'er

You're out and about - at work, and attending events and shows - but you still need to keep in touch with customers and the business. Here's the essential tech toolkit for the 5 to 9'er who has to spend hours away from the home office.

Email

A webmail system allows access to emails from anywhere. Have ready access to your archive of email wherever you go, on the home office computer, on your laptop on the move and even on your mobile phone. Gmail (www.google.com/mail) is a strong contender as it's free to use, has enormous storage capacity and is super-speedy, but there are others including Windows Live Hotmail (www.hotmail.com) and Yahoo! Mail (http://uk.mail.yahoo.com).

Remote desktop

Access your files and folders with GoToMyPC from Citrix Systems (www.gotomypc.com) or WebEx's PCnow (pcnow.webex.com) and take the business with you by utilising a web-based office system like Google Apps (www.google.com/apps) or Open Office (www.openoffice.org).

Telecoms

There is a host of cost-effective options to ensure you're available when you need to be, and delivering the right impression to clients:

- Follow-me number – Choose a number and direct calls to your landline or mobile. The beauty of choosing a number is you have the option to select either a freephone or a geographical number so, say, you'd like to have a Manchester area code, simply buy a number starting with 0161. The same goes for hundreds of other locations. Route calls to your mobile and choose a local number in any of 21 countries to have a virtual local presence with Skype (www.skype.com). Offer virtual phone numbers where the caller pays a local rate, regardless of where you are through Vonage (www.vonage.co.uk). Direct calls to you from a chosen number using internet technology and a virtual receptionist via eReceptionist (www.ereceptionist.co.uk).

- Smart phone – Respond to emails on the move with a smartphone or PDA (personal digital assistant). The BlackBerry (www.blackberry.com) and iPhone (www.apple.com/iphone) come out as preferred choices amongst 5 to 9'ers, for their performance and range of applications.

Right on time

When time is your most precious asset, you'll want to plan it, track it, and definitely make the most of it. Do so with these on and offline solutions.

Freshbooks
An application that tracks the time you spend on projects and turns this into professional looking invoices. Particularly useful for 5 to 9'ers providing professional and business services. www.freshbooks.com

PiBiDi
Access your calendar whilst on the move, plus customers can view your available appointments and book with you directly www.pibidi.com

Remember the milk
Take your task list with you and add to it from anywhere with this nifty web-based task manager that synchs with Google Calendar, Twitter, BlackBerry, iPhone, instant messenger, email and text messages. The basic package is free. www.rememberthemilk.com

Other time tracking software:
- Cashboard www.getcashboard.com
- Four Four Time www.fourfourtime.co.uk
- TraxTime www.spudcity.com/traxtime

- If, like me, you're still a pen-and-paper person invest in a diary, filofax or wall calendar from a wide range of options at shops such as www.staples.co.uk

- Keep track of family plans with the Family Joggler yourfamily.o2.co.uk/o2familyjoggler

Fed up of receiving those 'you weren't in' cards from the postman, requiring a trip to the collection point? Have parcels delivered to the pub! www.useyourlocal.com

And watch TV on your own time schedule:
- Channel 4 www.channel4.com/4od
- BBC www.bbc.co.uk/iplayer
- ITV www.itv.com/player
- Sky+ www.sky.com

A home on the web

People are starting to hear about you. That's great, but what would you like them to do about it? Each piece of company promotion should have a clear call to action – the simplest being to direct people to your website so they can take a step closer to becoming a customer.

Domain and hosting

The name of your business will influence your website (or domain) name (or possibly the other way round as it's best to see if a domain is available before naming the company). The domain makes up the main part of your website and email address, e.g. www.**enterprisenation**.com. As you'll be quoting the address to people quite a bit, choose a name that is:

- Simple
- Easy to remember
- Ideally, doesn't include numbers or dashes that you'll have to explain

Most domain registration companies also offer web space and hosting. This is the space to which you'll upload your web pages and pictures. It's best to be future-ready and book 1 or 2 GB (gigabyte) of web space for when your site traffic starts to take off. There are lots of companies that offer this service, and here are just a few to start you off:

- 1&1 www.oneandone.co.uk
- 123-reg www.123-reg.co.uk
- Easily.co.uk www.easily.co.uk

Once you've bought your name, you need to build your site. There are a number of options you can take.

Site essentials
Whichever route you decide to take be sure to include these key pages:

- About us
- Products/services
- News
- Contact us

DIY

Create your own
Hire a web design agency or enlist friends or family if you're lucky enough to know someone willing and able to help. Be clear on how you want the site to look, what you want it to do (now and in the future) and the kind of experience you'd like your visitor to have. Write this down in the form of a site specification and use this as a working guide with your chosen developer.

Template sites
A growing number of 5 to 9'ers (especially those who sell online) are turning to template sites as they offer great design teamed with e-commerce capability, built-in search engine optimisation and hosting. The various options available are displayed on pages 199-200.

Platform sites
Particularly relevant for the craft and handmade sector - rather than creating your own site, display products and sell your items via sales platform sites, including those outlined on pages 67-72.

The power of a professional image
When using images on your site you'll want to do so in the best light possible. A suggestion made in the Enterprise Nation forum by top poster, Gee Ranasinha, is to get hold of a light tent. They can be bought from professional photographic retailers, or make one yourself, Gee suggests, with this handy DIY guide: http://digital-photography-school.com/how-to-make-a-inexpensive-light-tent

Another option is to buy professional images, either from stock libraries or direct from photographers. A few examples are:

- www.imagesource.com
- www.istockphoto.com
- www.packshotfactory.com
- www.prodoto.com

Website builders

Product	Price	Features
Actinic www.actinic.co.uk	Actinic Express £1 set-up fee and £18 per month thereafter	Company has been established in UK since 1996 and has built solid reputation. Free 30 day trial on offer.
CubeCart www.cubecart.com	From free to £110, depending on the features required (cubecart.com/features)	E-commerce shopping cart used by more than 1 million store owners – so they must be doing something right! Free 30 day trial on offer.
Mr Site www.mrsite.com	3 packages: • £19.99 Beginner • £34.99 Standard • £99.99 Professional	Used by a good number of home businesses and 5 to 9'ers, you can buy the product in boxed or email format. Helpful tips on how to start via the site.
osCommerce www.oscommerce.com	Free	An open source solution with, to date, over 5,800 add-ons available for free to customise your store and increase sales.
Serif WebPlus serif.com/webplus	£79.99	There's an easy wizard to set up your store and choice of payment providers, including PayPal.
Shopcreator www.shopcreator.co.uk	3 packages ranging from %age of sales each month, to set fee of £90 per month for full retail features	Set up your site in minutes and benefit from the email/telephone support plus online forums.

Product	Price	Features
Shopify www.shopify.com	Starts with a basic package priced at £15 per month. The company recommends their 'business' package with full e-commerce capability at £60 per month	A hosted system that can link in a number of payment options with an admin section that allows easy management of orders. The company offers a free 30 day trial.
SitesPlus www.sitesplus.co.uk	£12.99 per month for standard package	Referral programme where you receive £10 of Sites Plus credit for referring friends and family.
Tradingeye www.tradingeye.com	£299 for a single license	A highly featured e-commerce package which comes with a simple template design.
WordPress e-commerce plug in instinct.co.nz/ e-commerce	Free for basic plug-in. Upgrade to Gold Cart to add more functionality for £25 (single blogger) and £120 (business)	WordPress with an ecommerce plugin. Comes complete with a tutorial on how to set up your store in less than 5 minutes.
Venda www.venda.com	£49.99 per month	The company has taken its powerful technology and platforms developed for retailers like Tesco, Sharp and Jimmy Choo, and applied it to help smaller businesses have a robust online presence.

All prices and offers correct at time of going to print.

Attracting traffic

Your fabulous new site is launched and your home on the web is open for business. Traffic is appearing on the back of the PR and media activity you're doing, so with a budget from a first batch of sales why not invest in a couple of online advertising options and measure the results to see what's working.

Pay per click (PPC) advertising
The steps laid out on pages 178-187 are designed to help you appear highly in search results when people look for the kind of product and service you offer.

These results will appear on the main engines (Google, Yahoo! and Bing) in the left column of the page as a natural or 'organic' search result. But have you spotted results on the right of the page when searching for items yourself? These are paid-for results and referred to as pay per click or PPC advertising.

PPC is where you pay to have ads displayed when people type in certain words, in the hope it will attract more visitors to your site. Here are two options to try on two of the largest sites in the world.

Facebook
Facebook has over 350 million users worldwide so if you need to be where your customers are, there's a good chance some of them will be here! By taking out Facebook Ads you can target demographics based on location, gender, marital status or even interests.

As an advertiser, you control how much you want to spend and set a daily budget. The minimum budget is US $1.00 (63p) a day. After designing the ad, decide for how long you want the campaign to run and whether you want to be charged for the number of clicks you receive (CPC) or the number of times your ad is displayed

TIP

Think like a buyer
When thinking of the keywords to use in PPC ad campaigns (and in search engine optimisation) think of the words your buyers will be using when searching for your product or service.

Use the Google AdWords Keyword Tool to find out the most popular search terms.

Apply these words in the campaign and include them in the text on your site.

(Cost per Impression or CPM). Wedding photographer, Chris Meyer, spent £190 on Facebook ads over a 2-year period and generated over £37,000 in new business. Impressive!

• www.facebook.com/advertising

Google

Google AdWords is another form of PPC advertising. Think of the key words or phrases you think your customers will be searching for and apply them in your Google campaign. Link to your home page or other pages on the site where you're running a promotion and make the most of Geotargeting, which lets you target your ads to specific territories and languages.

As with Facebook you are in full control of the budget and campaign duration. To get started, Google often runs promotions with partner companies to offer free AdWords vouchers. Look out for them and give Google Ads a go.

• adwords.google.co.uk

TIP

Search engines love links
Another way to increase your ranking in the search results is to link to other sites and vice versa but think quality here as opposed to quantity.

Sites offering the best 'link juice' are trusted domains, such as news sites, and very popular sites. You could post comments on such sites and blogs and include a link back to your site. Also try these handy hints:

• Approach sites complementary to your own and suggest reciprocal links.
• Ensure your website link is included in all your social media profiles [see pages 205-206].
• Register with the major search engines [see page 26].
Add your domain to local search services such as Google Maps, Qype, Yahoo local and BView
• www.google.co.uk/maps
• www.qype.co.uk
• www.uk.local.yahoo.com
• www.bview.co.uk

Measure the results

Time to measure what's working and what's not. You'll be pleased to know there's a whole host of tools that are free to use and will show real-time results for your site. Look out, in particular, for your traffic's source (which are your highest referring sites) and most popular pages. You can see days where your site receives spikes in visitor levels (and track this back to marketing) and measure if visitors are spending longer periods on the site and which times are popular, e.g. weekends, evenings, lunchtimes, etc.

Google Analytics offers intelligence on your website traffic and marketing effectiveness www.google.com/analytics

If you're concerned that just too much is being placed in the hands of Google, there are other options.

- **Alexa** Web traffic metrics, site demographics and top url listings: www.alexa.com
- **Clicky** Monitors and analyses your site traffic in real time: www.getclicky.com
- **Crazy Egg** See which pages visitors are visiting with a colourful heat map: www.crazyegg.com
- **Opentracker** Gather and analyse web stats and monitor online visitors: www.opentracker.net
- **StatCounter** An invisible web tracker and hit counter that offers data in real time: www.statcounter.com
- **Urchin** This is the tool we use to measure and monitor traffic to Enterprise Nation. It is now owned by Google!: www.urchin.com
- **Website Grader** Generates a free marketing report that compares your site with a competitor's: www.websitegrader.com

Hopefully what you will see is an upward curve of visitors and time spent on the site. If you're selling anything, then hopefully this means more sales. And if your site is the business, this means you're in a strong position to attract advertisers and begin doing affiliate deals [see pages 44-46].

TIP

Show me your rates!

The purpose of a media rate card is to show potential advertisers what your site can deliver to them in terms of traffic and sales. To do this, include some key points:

- **A brief description** of the site: What it does and for whom
- **Visitor demographics**: Do you have data on the age of your site visitors, their home region, gender, etc? If so, include, as it helps build a picture of your audience
- **Site traffic**: What are your unique visitor numbers and length of time spent on the site? Make a note if the figures are increasing
- **Costings**: Do you have a cost per click (CPC) or cost per impression (CPM) rate? If so, include it here, along with the price of other sponsorship options. Offer a menu but leave some flexibility with 'costed on a project basis' for sponsor features that would benefit from a more tailored proposal
- **Screen shots** of how and where adverts or sponsored features appear on the site
- **Media activity**: Note where you've recently been covered in the media, online and off, so potential sponsors can see how and where you're promoting the site
- **Testimonials**: Positive comments from existing sponsors gives you credibility and gives confidence to the next potential sponsor
- **Team details**: Who are the faces behind the site and what are your credentials, i.e. background career and activities

Round this off with your contact details so interested potential sponsors can get in touch and place an order!

Keep visitors coming back (also known as ... make my site sticky!)

Traffic is increasing and new visitors are finding the site. The aim now is to encourage return and repeat visits from those wanting to look, buy, read or interact. Achieve this by making yours a sticky site. Here's how.

Fresh content

If yours is a blog, try to post regularly, and if it's an e-commerce site, keep the product range updated. Give your site some TLC each day as fresh content will attract visitors who want to see what's new and will also appeal to the trawling web spiders who determine search engine results.

User-generated content

Encourage your site visitors to get to know each other through a forum, comment boxes or a plug-in application such as Webjam (www.webjam.com). Before you know it a sense of community will develop and visitors will log on each day to find out who's saying what and what's happening with whom.

Exclusive offers

Extend offers to your existing customers, readers or members that will tempt them back. This offer could be conditional on customers referring a friend: that way your customer returns to the site with others in tow. Add to this with a badge of honour; design a badge that visitors can display on their own site to show their affiliation to you.

TIP

Spread the word
Make it easy for visitors to spread word of your site through social sharing. Have your site Stumbled, Dugg and Tweeted and make the most of this viral effect. You can add these social bookmarking tools by visiting AddThis (addthis.com) and choose the icons you'd like to have displayed on your site.

The most popular are:

- Delicious
  delicious.com
- Digg
  digg.com
- StumbleUpon
  stumbleupon.com
- Twitter
  twitter.com

TIP

Flippin brilliant
Buy a Flip video camera (around £90) and simply press one button to start recording. It's as light as an iPod so can travel with you and, together with a Gorillapod tripod, can be used to record interviews with happy customers... or just about anything you fancy. Upload to your site and promote to visitors.

- Flip
  theflip.com
- Gorillapod
  joby.com/
  gorillapod

TIP

Follow me!
Remember to include your Twitter, Facebook, website address, etc in your email signature. Also add the Twitter, Facebook, YouTube, etc icons to your site to encourage followers.

Pictures and videos

Experiment a little. Upload photos of people and products to the site so it offers visitors a reason to stay a while and gaze. Then step it up with some video content. Upload recordings of you producing your work or customers enjoying your work. Do this cost-effectively (and simply) with a Flip camera.

Guest appearances

Invite special guests to appear on your site, via guest blog posts, hosting a webchat, or a featured interview.

Content, but not as we know it

Got some content to share but aware your visitors don't have enormous amounts of time to read it? Why not present your expertise in the form of an online slide show using Slideshare (www.slideshare.net) or produce a podcast with Garageband software on the Mac (www.apple.com/ilife/garageband).

Keep in touch

Communicate all these good and sticky things to your users through a regular e-newsletter powered by products such as MailChimp (www.mailchimp.com), AWeber Communications (www.aweber.com) or Mailshots Online from Royal Mail (www.mailshotsonline.co.uk).

Look the part
(not the part-timer)

If you don't want them to, no one need know the business is a part-time affair. Create a professional image from the moment calls are answered, through to meeting clients and contacts.

Your own PA

When working by day, it's hard to take each call. The good news is someone else can do it for you and create a professional image, as the phone is answered by a PA who knows your business and your schedule. The company that delivers a superior service in this area is Moneypenny.

- alldayPA www.alldaypa.com
- Answer www.answer.co.uk
- Moneypenny www.moneypenny.co.uk @moneypennyPA

Virtually anywhere

Don't want to use your home address? Invest in a virtual office that entitles you to a professional postal address and a service where the host company will send on your post, or enable you to collect it. There are a number of providers (see below) but the one that offers the greatest selection of UK (and international) options is Regus.

Virtual office providers
- Mail Boxes Etc. www.mbe.co.uk
- Regus www.regus.com
- Virtual Office Group www.voffice.com
- Your City Office www.yourcityoffice.com

Meet at my place, or yours?

If you'd rather not have clients and contacts coming to your home for meetings, or you need a location that's more convenient for your contact, become a member of a club, office network or hub facility. Here are a few:

eOffice

Provides office space, meeting rooms and virtual offices in 100 locations across 30 countries

* www.eoffice.net

Enterprise Nation

Find your local homeworking hub facility as we profile the spaces and places in your area providing services to 5 to 9'ers

* www.enterprisenation.com

One Alfred Place

A first class facility for 5 to 9'ers based in London or those needing a professional meeting place in the city

* www.onealfredplace.com

Regus

Their membership cards gain access to a global network of over 1000 business centres across 450 cities in 75 countries.

* www.regus.com

See page 132 for other hub facilities across the UK.

Time-saving techniques

The business is growing and time has become your most precious resource. Is it time, therefore, to consider outsourcing some of the tasks you do? Free yourself up to dedicate your attention to sales, strategy ... or even catching up with the latest episode of *Spooks*!

What can be outsourced, and to whom?

Admin
Hire a VA (virtual PA) to do the admin tasks you don't want or have the time to do. Visit VA directories and resources (listed on page 23) to find your perfect match.

PR, marketing and design
Outsource your PR to a specialist who can be pitching and promoting the business whilst you're at work. Find skilled professionals on directory sites such as PeoplePerHour (www.peopleperhour.com) and Business Smiths (www.businesssmiths.co.uk). For one-off design projects visit 99 Designs (www.99designs.com) or Wooshii (www.wooshii.com).

Sales
Hire a sales expert to make calls, set up appointments and attend trade shows. Moneypenny (mentioned on page 207) also offers an outbound sales call service, or try Physis (www.physis-consulting.com) a specialist in matching freelance sales consultants with relevant companies.

Telemarketing/outbound sales calls
* Moneypenny www.moneypenny.co.uk
* Great Guns www.greatgunsmarketing.co.uk
* 365 Group www.365direct.co.uk

Fulfilment

You went into business to do what you enjoy. So, unless it's your thing, I expect you're wondering why you're spending time on picking 'n' packing? Let someone else take care of fulfilment. Services like myWarehouse offer outsourced fulfilment for any quantity; perfect for the 5 to 9'er starting out with a few orders.

Brent Shaw is a 5 to 9'er and MD of online business, SwissLuggage.com. He's also a customer of myWarehouse:

"As you can imagine it was a tough decision to outsource as it's like giving your child to someone else to look after – this was our baby and it was very important that we felt someone else would continue to manage our pick, pack and ship solution in the same way and with the same expectations we had set out. 5 months on, we are happy, orders have risen month on month and we have been able to focus on further developing the Swiss Luggage brand."

- www.mywarehouse.me

Customer service

Looking after your customers is vital, but even that can be outsourced to great effect. Get Satisfaction's tagline is 'people-powered customer service' – it provides a web-hosted platform, much like a forum, where customers can ask questions, suggest improvements, report a problem or give praise. It can save you time and money by making customer service an open process that leverages the wisdom of crowds. Questions are answered by other users, rather than you as the site host.

You don't want to outsource this completely as it's good to show personal contact with customers, but this is a useful tool that could improve your business as customers offer their feedback.

- www.getsatisfaction.com

IT

Research from Virgin Digital Help reveals that home-business owners spend almost 3 hours trying to fix a single IT problem, and a quarter are spending over £20 a month trying to get technology to work properly. Outsource the hassle and save your time, money and blood pressure.

- www.virgindigitalhelp.co.uk

TIP

The beauty of barter

Many 5 to 9'ers barter their goods and services, e.g. I'll produce a sales brochure for you, in exchange for a handmade cushion for my living room.

This works well as both parties get what they want but take heed of the tax implications. Bartering means money doesn't show up in your accounts. But there has been an exchange of goods and services, which implies a taxable activity. The taxman could view bartering as a way to avoid tax but with so many beneficial arrangements underway, maybe it's time to revise the tax situation.

Accounts

Unless you are in the accountancy business, this is almost a must to be outsourced. Monthly payroll, accounts, VAT returns and corporate tax returns all take time and it's time you can't afford or simply don't have. A cost/benefit analysis is likely to show that it's cheaper to outsource to a qualified accountant.

Ask around for recommendations of accountants in your area who deliver a quality service at a competitive cost.

For bookkeeping services it may be worth checking out Rosemary Bookkeeping (www.rosemarybookkeeping.com), a franchised business with a growing network of bookkeepers.

For online accounting and invoicing that makes life easier for you and your accountant, check out:

- Crunch www.crunch.co.uk
- FreeAgent www.freeagentcentral.com
- KashFlow www.kashflow.co.uk
- Liquid www.liquidaccounts.net
- QuickBooks www.quickbooks.co.uk
- TAS Software www.tassoftware.co.uk

And for useful tips on accounting changes and updates for part-time and home-based businesses, visit 1st Addition Accountancy blog (1staddition.blogspot.com).

Do what you do best and outsource the rest – steps to successful outsourcing

Do the groundwork

Spend some time working on the task yourself so you've built some foundations before handing it over to a third party. For example, if you outsource sales then have a ready-made contacts list and some open doors that the specialist can build on, rather than starting from scratch. This will make it more cost-effective for you and means they hit the ground running; it's not a contract from a cold start, you have already done the groundwork.

Be clear on the brief

Having spent some time doing the task yourself, you will have a clear idea of the brief. Back to the example of outsourcing sales, if you've spent 6-12 months sourcing leads and making contacts, you'll have a much clearer idea of the type of prospecting the specialist should do. The clearer the brief, the better the results.

Take your time

And take references. Spend time evaluating the specialists in the market and, if you can, talk to their existing clients. Do they have the industry experience you're after? Will they represent your brand in a professional manner? Have they shown commitment to other clients? When an outsourced arrangement works well, the partner becomes part of your team so choose them as carefully as you would choose an employee.

Let go!

Outsourcing a key function means having to let go a little. Someone else becomes accountable for these results. Embrace this rather than resist it. As the business owner you remain in ultimate control but the expert will need their own space in which to flourish.

Outsourcing can save you time and help make you money. Finding the right partner, on the right terms, will make you feel like a new and liberated person.

Team work

Once you've chosen your outsourced partner(s), it's important to keep in regular contact and work together as a team. There are a number of online project management and collaboration tools to help you stay on top of projects and in control of the company.

Basecamp

The project management tool we rely on at Enterprise Nation. This is a top-class product that allows you to create projects, invite people to view them, upload files and make comments. It's effective online project management that can be accessed from anywhere.

- www.basecamphq.com

GoogleDocs

Share documents via Google with GoogleDocs. You can edit on the move, choose who accesses documents and share changes in real-time.

- docs.google.com

Two tools not yet tried and tested by the Enterprise Nation team:

Glasscubes
This tool offers project management, collaboration and CRM (Customer Relationship Management) all in one package.
- www.glasscubes.com

Huddle
Offers simple and secure online workspaces. Huddle is hosted so there's no software to download and it's free to get started.
- www.huddle.net

Solutions to enable group-talk:

Dimdim
Attend live meetings, demonstrations and webinars
- www.dimdim.com

Ketchup
Share and record meeting notes
- www.useketchup.com

Pow Wow Now
Free conference calling at 'Open Access' level. Priced packages available
- www.powwownow.co.uk

Skype
Free and easy to use conference calls for Skype users
- www.skype.com/allfeatures/conferencecall

Tinychat
Group video conferencing, for free
- www.tinychat.com

The golden triangle

As the business continues to grow, bear in mind the golden triangle that will keep you and the business in balance. This requires spending roughly a third of your time on 3 key things:

1. **Customer care**
   Taking care of the customers you have with good service, regular communication and an innovative line of products and services.

2. **Business development**
   Secure new clients through marketing, encouraging recommendations and direct-sales calls and pitches.

3. **Admin**
   Not as enjoyable as the first 2, but it still has to be done. Keep the books in order by raising invoices in good time, being on top of cash flow and filing tax returns and company documents on time and in order.

And finally … Creating your own private Idaho

When working by day and returning home to grow the business at night, you'll want to feel comfortable and content in your 5 to 9 surroundings. Follow this checklist to create the perfect work environment.

Find dedicated space

Try to create an area in the house that functions as your dedicated workspace. That way you can mentally adjust yourself to be in business mode when in that space. It could be a spare room, in the attic, under the stairs or even the garden shed. For garden office dwellers, one blog you will like is Shedworking (www.shedworking.co.uk).

Invest in a good desk and chair

Depending on the nature of your business you could be spending a few hours each day at the desk and in your chair, so be sure they're sturdy and comfortable! Ideally, your feet should be flat on the floor with your knees at 90 degrees. Your back should be straight, and not hunched over the keyboard.

A light touch

Lots of light is good for your mood and work pace but avoid too much task-light shining on the computer monitor. As for colours on the walls, go for light shades as they will make the space look bigger, and consider mirrors to bounce light around.

Double-up

Invest in storage boxes and turn your wardrobes into filing cabinets! Or buy big boxes, label them well and then find a place to hide them away; maybe doubling up as a chair for visitors.

TIP

A few ace accessories

With earnings coming in from the business, why not treat yourself to a couple of gizmos and gadgets that will make 5 to 9 working that much more appealing?

You Me Wall Clock – Write on and affix multiple hands to this 24 hour clock face that designates the time zones of your favourite places.
- www.nexus-publishing.co.uk/wordpress/archives/926

One Less Desk – If pushed for space at home, this slide-away desk could be the answer.
- www.nexus-publishing.co.uk/wordpress/archives/306

Biscuit Mug – Keep a stock of biscuits safe and stored in this very clever mug.
- www.nexus-publishing.co.uk/wordpress/archives/379

Biorb – What more could a 5 to 9'er wish for than an office aquarium that provides a 24 hour light cycle, including natural sunrise, sunset and blue moonlight?
- www.nexus-publishing.co.uk/wordpress/archives/372

Aerogarden – If flora and fauna are more your thing, bring the outdoors indoors with this self-contained garden. The good thing is, it's scientifically proven that having plants in your home office helps with humidity levels and dust, and reduces any sense of isolation.
- www.nexus-publishing.co.uk/wordpress/archives/92

From the Desk Litter blog

Have a vision

Put a vision board up on the wall and on it stick pictures that represent your personal and business ambitions; places you want to visit, targets for the company, and people with whom you enjoy spending time. Glance at it each day to remind yourself of everything you're working towards.

Roam free

Install wi-fi so it's possible to work from anywhere. To get started you need a wireless router which you may have received free from your Internet Service Provider (ISP). If not, check out respectable suppliers such as Netgear (www.netgear.co.uk).

Surround sound

A great benefit of having your own workspace is that you can play (and dance to) your favourite tunes. As for speakers, our tech editor, San Sharma, recommends JBL Creature II speakers which "look good and sound great" (www.jbl.com).

Conclusion

I hope this book has filled you with inspiration.

With it in hand you have your guide to turn your idea into a business.

Make the most of your 5 to 9 time by utilising technology tools and gadgets, promote your venture for free, and plot a future where you're earning from doing something you love.

Individual stories of 5 to 9'ers paint a picture of people happily realising their ambitions:

"Running my own business offers such great freedom that it often does not feel like work!"
Dolapo James, Urban Knit

"Piddley Pix was born from a hobby, and what would be better than having a full-time job getting paid to do my hobby – that would be fantastic!"
Kelly Brett, Piddley Pix

"Setting up and developing a business whilst being in full-time employment and also ensuring time for myself, partner and friends is tough but this is life, it's busy and that's when it's exciting!"
Janan Leo, CocoRose London

"One of the major benefits of running your own business is that you can control your direction and make your own decisions."
David Sandy, Integreat Media

You too can realise these benefits and this book shows you how. Take it with you as you embark on your first steps and visit Enterprise Nation to ask questions in our forums, stay in touch with business ideas and techniques, or just have a natter with us at #watercoolermoment on Twitter! However you decide to access the site, you'll discover a community of friends to help you along the way.

So don't give up the day job (just yet) – start by Working 5 to 9!

Emma Jones
Enterprise Nation

twitter.com/e_nation
twitter.com/emmaljones

FAQs

Here's a summary of all you need to know on the admin side of working 5 to 9.

Do I tell the taxman I'm working 5 to 9?

Yes. As soon as you start earning, register with HM Revenue & Customs to declare your earnings.

Do I tell my employer I'm working 5 to 9?

Probably best to, yes. Most 5 to 9'ers profiled have informed their employer and the response has been positive. After all, your employer benefits from all the new entrepreneurial skills you're picking up at nights and weekends. However, you should first check your terms of employment to check any restrictions on you having other jobs whilst employed.

Do I tell my insurance provider?

Yes. It's likely you will have a (perhaps second or third) computer in the house and possibly some stock. If so, you want to ensure this is protected. If you have clients or contacts visiting the house, you'll need public liability insurance (you'll also need this when displaying at craft fairs, farmers' markets, etc) and if you're providing business services, you'll need professional indemnity insurance. It's not expensive to add these on to your existing home insurance, or you can buy an all-in-one home business package.

Should I set up a business bank account?

When first starting out, it's not compulsory to set up a business bank account but it is advisable as it keeps records clear and separate from the start.

Will I need to borrow or raise money to start my business?

It depends on the nature of your business and what your upfront costs are. Very few of the featured 5 to 9'ers needed to raise money as their salary provided the start-up funds they needed and the subsequent sales provided the cash flow to keep the business going.

How much can I earn from working 5 to 9?

As little or as much as you like! That's the beauty of starting a business by working 5 to 9 – you have the freedom and flexibility to choose whether you'd like to keep the business as a spare-time venture or to ramp things up so it fills your time and your bank account.

When will I know to go full-time?

This is probably a financial decision. When you're earning enough from the business or when you think the business won't grow anymore without you being able to give it the time, then maybe it's time to wave goodbye to employment and say hello to full-on self-employment. Only you will know when it's right for you and your circumstances.

Will this be the best move I've ever made?

Absolutely!

And if you do give up the day job, then be sure to leave on good terms – your employer could become an important client of your new business!

Working 5 to 9

Written by Alan Law, www.give-a-song.com

Verse 1:
Sitting at my desk,
And doing the same thing,
Wearing my suit, waiting for the phone to ring,
Every day just doing this all the time.
But there is a way
To make things better,
Where I can choose to work in a sweater –
Working for myself, from 5 to 9.

Chorus:
Working 5 to 9,
Your own business in your spare time,
What I make is mine,
You know there's no ladder to climb,
I am my own boss,
Only making my own coffee,
It's a dream that I can turn into reality!
5 to 9,
It don't feel like working really,
'Cause I'm doing my
Passion or my hobby,
And for just these few
Hours that I'm giving,
I'm turning what I love into a living!

Verse 2:
Everything I do,
I'll do it for me,
Deciding what's best for my own company,
No-one to tell me what to do!
If I want to earn more,
You can bet I'll make it,
If I want a break, well, yes, I'll take it,
'Cause I'm working for myself, and not you!

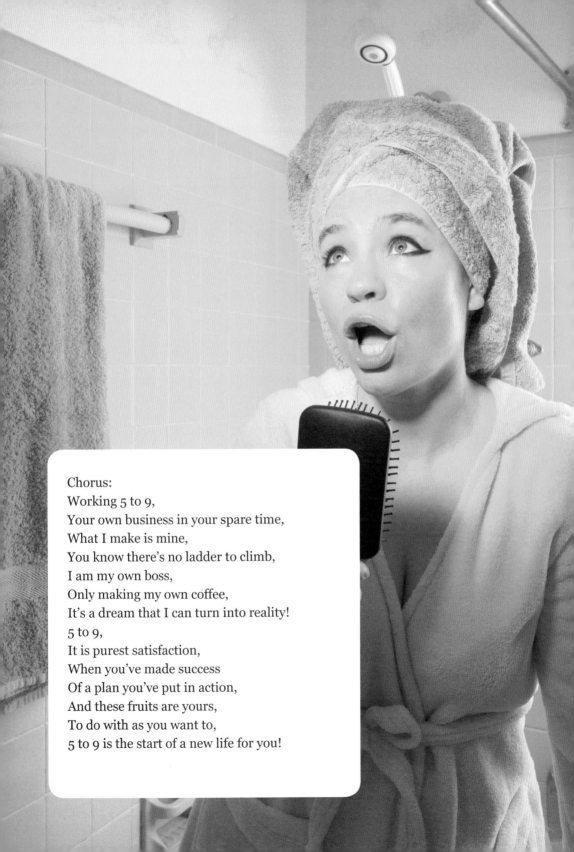

Chorus:
Working 5 to 9,
Your own business in your spare time,
What I make is mine,
You know there's no ladder to climb,
I am my own boss,
Only making my own coffee,
It's a dream that I can turn into reality!
5 to 9,
It is purest satisfaction,
When you've made success
Of a plan you've put in action,
And these fruits are yours,
To do with as you want to,
5 to 9 is the start of a new life for you!

Useful links

Enterprise Nation

The UK's most popular resource for anyone starting and growing a business from home www.enterprisenation.com

Artisan and craft sites and resources

The Affordable Vintage Fair www.vintagefair.co.uk

All Things Original www.allthingsoriginal.com

ArtFire www.artfire.com

Buy Handmade www.buyhandmade.org

Coriandr www.coriandr.com

Crafty Blogs www.craftyblogs.co.uk

DaWanda www.dawanda.com

Dreamaid www.dreamaid.com

Etsy www.etsy.com

Folksy.com www.folksy.com

Freeosk www.freeosk.co.uk

Gift Wrapped & Gorgeous www.giftwrappedandgorgeous.co.uk

Glasgow Craft Mafia www.glasgowcraftmafia.com

GlimpseOnline www.glimpseonline.com

Handmade Craft Fairs www.handmadecraftfairs.co.uk

Joolia www.joolia.com

The Make Lounge www.themakelounge.com

Makers Online www.makers-online.co.uk

MISI www.misi.co.uk

MyEhive www.myehive.com

Not mass produced www.notmassproduced.com

NotOnTheHighStreet www.notonthehighstreet.com

Nottingham Craft Mafia www.nottinghamcraftmafia.com

Project Wonderful www.projectwonderful.com

Sheffield's Craft Consortium www.craft-candy.org

Shop Handmade UK www.shophandmade.co.uk

UK Handmade www.ukhandmade.co.uk

We Make London wemakelondon.blogspot.com

Blogging platforms

Blogger www.blogger.com

Live Journal www.livejournal.com

Vox www.vox.com

WordPress www.wordpress.com

Blogging tips & income streams

Amazon Affiliates affiliate-program.amazon.co.uk

Become A Blogger www.becomeablogger.com

Copyblogger www.copyblogger.com

Google AdSense www.google.com/adsense

IZEA www.izea.com

TextLinkAds www.text-link-ads.com

Blogging associations

British Mummy Bloggers www.britishmummybloggers.co.uk

Crafty Blogs www.craftyblogs.co.uk

Travel BlogCamp www.travelblogcamp.co.uk

UK Food Bloggers Association www.ukfba.co.uk

Business awards

Awards Intelligence www.awardsintelligence.co.uk

Business services

99designs www.99designs.com

Business Smiths www.businesssmiths.co.uk

Elance.com www.elance.com

Gumtree www.gumtree.com

PeoplePerHour www.peopleperhour.com

SetYourRate www.setyourrate.com

Wooshii www.wooshii.com

Business support

Business Link www.businesslink.gov.uk

Enterprise UK www.enterpriseuk.org

NFEA www.nfea.com

PRIME www.primeinitiative.co.uk

Domain registrants & hosting providers

1&1 www.oneandone.co.uk

123-reg www.123-reg.co.uk

Go Daddy www.godaddy.com

Heart Internet www.heartinternet.co.uk

Low Cost Names www.lowcostnames.co.uk

eBay advice

eBay sell.ebay.co.uk/sell

eBay UK Bulletin www.ebaybulletin.co.uk

Tame Bay www.tamebay.com

Vendlab www.vendlab.com

Vzaar www.vzaar.com

Email tools & marketing

Google Mail www.google.com/mail

Hotmail www.hotmail.com

Yahoo! Mail uk.mail.yahoo.com

AWeber www.aweber.com

MailChimp www.mailchimp.com

Mailshots Online www.mailshotsonline.co.uk

Farmers' markets

Farmers' Markets www.farmersmarkets.net

Virtual Farmers Market www.vfmuk.com

Free directories

Approved Index www.approvedindex.co.uk

B2B Index www.b2bindex.co.uk

Brownbook www.brownbook.net

FreeIndex www.freeindex.co.uk

SearchSight www.searchsight.com

UK Directory List www.ukdirectorylist.co.uk

WeCanDo www.wecando.biz

Fulfilment providers

myWarehouse www.mywarehouse.me

Graduate resources

Enternships www.enternships.com

FlyingStart www.flyingstartonline.com

National Consortium of University Entrepreneurs (NACUE) www.nacue.com

National Council for Graduate Entrepreneurship www.ncge.com

School for Startups www.schoolforstartups.co.uk

Shell LiveWIRE www.shell-livewire.org

Health & safety

Health and Safety Executive www.hse.gov.uk

Cosmetic Safety Assessment www.cosmeticsafetyassessment.com

Council inspection (local) www.direct.gov.uk

Home business opportunities

Arbonne www.arbonneinternational.co.uk

Avon www.avon.com

Flori Roberts www.floriroberts.co.uk

Funky Feet www.funkyfeetunlimited.co.uk

Girlie Gardening www.girliegardening.com

House Tutor www.housetutor.co.uk

Jamie at Home www.jamieathome.com

Kleeneze www.kleeneze.net

MusicBugs www.musicbugs.co.uk

My Little Wrapper www.getmylittlewrapper.co.uk

My Secret Kitchen www.mysecretkitchen.co.uk

The Pampered Chef www.pamperedchef.co.uk

Tish Tash Toys www.tishtashtoys.com

Usborne Books www.usborne.com

VIE at home www.vieathome.com

Hub facilities

Electricworks www.electric-works.net

Enterprise HQ www.enterprise-hq.co.uk

eOffice www.eoffice.net

Forward Space www.forwardspace.co.uk

FunkBunk www.funkbunk.com

The Hub www.the-hub.net

Huddersfield Media Centre www.the-media-centre.co.uk

Indycube www.indycube.biz

Leicester Creative Business Depot www.lcbdepot.co.uk

Space on Tap www.spaceontap.com

Third Door www.third-door.com

Watershed www.watershed.co.uk

Image libraries

Alamy www.alamy.com

Fotolia www.fotolia.com

fotoLibra www.fotolibra.com

Getty Images www.gettyimages.com

Image Source www.imagesource.com

iStockphoto www.istockphoto.com

Packshot Factory www.packshotfactory.com

Prodoto www.prodoto.com

IT support

Virgin Digital Help www.virgindigitalhelp.co.uk

Meeting space/members club

eOffice www.eoffice.net

One Alfred Place www.onealfredplace.com

Regus www.regus.com

Networking groups

1230 TWC www.1230.co.uk

4Networking www.4networking.biz

The Athena Network www.theathenanetwork.com

British Chambers of Commerce www.britishchambers.org.uk

Business Scene www.business-scene.com

Ecademy www.ecademy.com

First Friday www.firstfriday-network.co.uk

Jelly www.workatjelly.com

School for Startups www.schoolforstartups.co.uk

She's Ingenious www.shesingenious.org

Women in Rural Enterprise (WiRE) www.wireuk.org

Online advertising

Facebook www.facebook.com/advertising

Google AdWords adwords.google.co.uk

Online scheduling

PiBiDi www.pibidi.com

Online translation

Language123 www.language123.com

Lingo24 www.lingo24.com

PA services

AlldayPA www.alldaypa.com

Answer www.answer.co.uk

EReceptionist www.ereceptionist.co.uk

Moneypenny www.moneypenny.co.uk

Parcel delivery service

Parcel2Go www.parcel2go.com

Payment provider

PayPal www.paypal.co.uk

Press release submission

Response Source www.responsesource.com

PR Newswire www.prnewswire.co.uk

PRWeb www.prweb.com

Project management & shared workspace

Basecamp www.basecamphq.com

Dimdim www.dimdim.com

Google Docs docs.google.com

Glasscubes www.glasscubes.com

Huddle www.huddle.net

Ketchup www.useketchup.com

Search engines

Bing www.bing.com

Google www.google.com

Yahoo! www.yahoo.com

Self-publishing

Blurb www.blurb.com

Lulu www.lulu.com

Newspaper Club www.newspaperclub.co.uk

The Twitter Times www.twittertim.es

Yudu www.yudu.com

Zmags www.zmags.co.uk

Self-storage

Access Self Storage www.accessselfstorage.com

Site analytics

Google Analytics www.google.com/analytics

Alexa www.alexa.com

Clicky www.getclicky.com

Crazy Egg www.crazyegg.com

Opentracker www.opentracker.net

StatCounter www.statcounter.com

Urchin www.urchin.com

Website Grader www.websitegrader.com

Social bookmarking

Add This www.addthis.com

Delicious www.delicious.com

Digg www.digg.com

StumbleUpon www.stumbleupon.com

Twitter www.twitter.com

Social enterprise

Social Enterprise Awards www.socialenterpriseawards.org.uk

Social Enterprise Coalition www.socialenterprise.org.uk

Social Enterprise Mark www.socialenterprisemark.co.uk

UnLtd www.unltd.org.uk

Social media

Facebook www.facebook.com

Flickr www.flickr.com

LinkedIn www.linkedin.com

Twitter www.twitter.com

YouTube www.youtube.com

Survey tools

SurveyMonkey www.surveymonkey.com

Task managers

Cashboard www.getcashboard.com

Four Four Time www.fourfourtime.co.uk

Remember the Milk www.rememberthemilk.com

TraxTime www.spudcity.com/traxtime

Tax

HM Revenue & Customs www.hmrc.gov.uk

Telecoms

BlackBerry www.blackberry.com

iPhone www.apple.com/iphone

Pow Wow Now www.powwownow.co.uk

Skype www.skype.com

Skype Conference call www.skype.com/allfeatures/conferencecall

Tinychat www.tinychat.com

Vonage www.vonage.co.uk

Trade bodies/associations

Association of Image Consultants International www.aici.org

Association of Online Publishers www.ukaop.org.uk

The Association of Photographers www.the-aop.org

Federation of Small Businesses www.fsb.org.uk

Forum of Private Business www.fpb.org

Guild of Craft Soap & Toiletry Makers www.gcstm.co.uk

Institute of Chartered Accountants in England & Wales www.icaew.com

International Association of Virtual Assistants www.iava.org.uk

International Federation of Image Consultants www.tfic.org.uk

Musicians Union www.musiciansunion.org.uk

Professional Contractors Group (PCG) www.pcg.org.uk

The Publishers Association www.publishers.org.uk

Society of Virtual Assistants www.societyofvirtualassistants.co.uk

Virtual Assistance Chamber of Commerce www.virtualassistantnetworking.com

The Writers Guild of Great Britain www.writersguild.org.uk

Trading platforms

BT Tradespace www.bttradespace.com

eBay www.ebay.co.uk

Training bodies

The Coaching Academy www.the-coaching-academy.com

Home Stagers www.homestagers.co.uk

Mums Who Bake www.mumswhobake.co.uk

Premier Training International www.premierglobal.co.uk

Soap School www.soapschool.com

Virtual offices

CityOffice www.yourcityoffice.com

Mail Boxes Etc. www.mbe.co.uk

Regus www.regus.com

The Virtual Office Group www.voffice.com

Website builders

Actinic www.actinic.co.uk

CubeCart www.cubecart.com

Mr Site www.mrsite.com

osCommerce www.oscommerce.com

Serif WebPlus www.serif.com/webplus

Shopcreator www.shopcreator.co.uk

Shopify www.shopify.com

SitesPlus www.sitesplus.co.uk

Tradingeye www.tradingeye.com

WordPress e-commerce plug-in www.instinct.co.nz/e-commerce

Venda www.venda.com

Profiled 5 to 9'ers

Lola Bailey	LifeWest9	www.lifewest9.co.uk/blog
John Batchelor	ur 1st car	www.ur1stcar.co.uk
Rob Birkett	LeavingLaw	www.leavinglaw.com
Kelly Brett	PiddleyPix	www.piddleypix.com
Michelle Briffa	Paragon Virtual Assistance	www.paragon-va.co.uk
Sharon Brooke & Ryan Smethurst	Urban Africa	www.urban-africa.co.uk
Claire Brown	Miso Funky	www.misofunky.com
Daniel Chapman & Carly Clarke	Twinkly Babies	www.twinklybabies.co.uk
Ruth Cheesley	Suffolk Computer Services	www.suffolkcomputerservices.co.uk
Anne Clarke	Angel Eden	www.angeleden.co.uk
Dave Clayton	Big Laces	www.biglaces.co.uk
Emily Coltman	Home Business Accountant	www.homebusinessaccountant.co.uk
Matt Conway	Conways Origami	www.conwaysorigami.com
Victoria Dixon	Enhance Me	www.enhance-me.com
Jonathan Dowden	Jonathan Mark Magic	www.jonathanmarkmagic.co.uk
Juliette Dyke	Fresh Air Fix	www.freshairfix.com
Harriet Easton	Harry's Beer	www.rushingdolls.com
Steve Emecz	MX Publishing	www.mxpublishing.co.uk
James Fletcher and Sharon Phillips	Unique Wildwood Furniture	www.uniquewildwoodfurniture.co.uk
Vernon Fuller	Vernon Fuller	www.vernonfuller.co.uk
Semona Glace	Home Stagers	www.homestagers.co.uk
Sarah and Andy Goodall	inkydeep	www.inkydeep.com
Louise Graham	Charming Angels	charmingangelsparties.co.uk
Paula Green	Kitty and Polly	www.kittyandpolly.co.uk
Arthur Guy	a star solutions	www.astarsolutions.co.uk
Diane Hall	The Writing Hall	www.thewritinghall.co.uk

Andy Hawkswell	Sweat Personal Training	www.sweatpersonaltraining.co.uk
Sue Hedges & Angela Savchenko	Moan about Men	www.moanaboutmen.com
Derek Houghton	Derek Houghton Images	www.derekhoughton-images.net
Gwen Howell	Pigs in Clover	www.pigsinclover.co.uk
Karyl Isles	Arbonne	www.arbonne.com
Dolapo James	Urban Knit	www.urbanknit.com
Cheryl Kelly	Precious Nappies	www.preciousnappies.co.uk
Nicola Kelsall	Spiralling	www.spiralling.co.uk
Mandy Key	Jamie at Home	www.jamieathome.com
Ola Laniyan-Amoako	Urbantopia	www.urbantopia.co.uk
Louise Land	Cirencester Cupcakes	www.cirencestercupcakes.com
Alan Law	Give A Song	www.give-a-song.com
Janan Leo	CocoRose London	www.cocoroselondon.com
Lynne Machin	Cheeky Moo	www.cheekymoo.com
Katie MacDonald	Virtually Does It	www.virtuallydoesit.com
Emma McCrory	Rock Face Minerals	www.rockfaceminerals.co.uk
Claire Melvin	Claire's Handmade Cakes	www.claireshandmadecakes.com
Julie Mitchell-Mehta	Fitnag	www.fitnag.com
Tracy O'Toole	Chrysalis Image	www.chrysalisimage.com
Beth Pagett	Buttercup Buttons	www.folksy.com/shops/butter-cupcreations
John Randall	JV Bouncy Castle Hire	www.bouncycastleshire.co.uk
Bill Rappos Kostas Eleftheriou, Vassilis Samolis	GreatApps Ltd	www.greatapps.co.uk
Tom Reader	Alver Valley Software	www.alvervalleysoftware.co.uk
Lezli and David Rees	Driving with Dogs	www.drivingwithdogs.co.uk
Terri Rhind	My Secret Kitchen	www.mysecretkitchen.co.uk
Rob Russell	Internet Marketing Solutions	www.imsuk.co.uk
David Sandy	Integreat Media	www.integreatmedia.com

Barbara Steadman	Another Gorgeous Day	www.anothergorgeousday.co.uk
Wendy Stott	Wendy Stott Translator	wendystott.language123.com
Caroline Taylor	Patchwork Harmony	www.patchworkharmony.co.uk
Lynn Taylor	Penelope Parasol	www.penelopeparasols.com
Kane Towning	AIM Clubbing	www.aimclubbing.co.uk
Andrew Wilcox	Readersheds	www.readersheds.co.uk
Kat Williams	Rock 'n Roll Bride	www.rocknrollbride.com
Haoming Yau	Promise Aid	www.promiseaid.com

What people are saying about Emma's first book,
Spare Room Start Up: How to start a business from home

"Fascinating, educational, practical, easy to read and understand."
- Valerie Dwyer,
My Wonderful Life Coach

"The book is gorgeous and very useful too. Lots of business books leave me cold, but this one is inspiring."
- Imperfectly Natural

"This book gives you all the pointers you need... Enormously helpful."
- Choice magazine's 'Financial Book of the Month'

"A cracking read."
- Shedworking

"A fantastic new book... [We] feel anyone thinking about the big step of starting their own business should go out now and buy this book."
- Seek It Out

"Spare Room Start Up *has a pedigree that is hard to fault... Your trusted companion on the adventure ahead."
- Homeworker

"Tycoons' tips to beat the credit crunch: Use your spare room to hit the jackpot."
- Daily Star

Daily Telegraph Business Club 'Book of the Week'
- 20th May 2008.

"A wonderful, concise, well written, fun to read collection of hints, tips, how-to's and case studies."
- Home Office Warrior

Waterstone's first Business Book of the Month
- May 2008

Emma Jones

Spare Room
START UP

How to start a business from home

Available at www.spareroomstartup.com
and all good book shops

Working

5 TO 9

www.working5to9.co.uk